D1171442

The English Abbey

F. H. CROSSLEY

Revised by

BRYAN LITTLE

B. T. BATSFORD LTD LONDON

First Paperback Edition 1962

For copyright reasons, this book may not be issued to the public on loan or otherwise except in its original soft cover.

PRINTED AND BOUND IN ENGLAND BY
HUNT, BARNARD AND CO. LTD., FOR THE PUBLISHERS
B. T. BATSFORD LTD.
4 FITZHARDINGE STREET, PORTMAN SQUARE, LONDON W.1

Reviser's Preface

This book, first published over a quarter of a century ago, has now been considerably altered both in matter and presentation. I have thought it helpful, for readers in the 1960s, to clarify its scope and explain how its subject has in some ways been amplified.

The main purpose of *The English Abbey* remains as it was. The book deals with the origins and life, and describes the churches and domestic buildings, of the religious orders which flourished in England and Wales before the Reformation. The "orders", some more centrally organised than others, were those whose vocation and work were primarily claustral—overwhelmingly centred in the church and in the domestic buildings immediately attached to it. As some establishments were ruled by abbots (or abbesses) and some by priors (or prioresses), and as the houses of the canons regular had little to distinguish them from those of the Benedictines, Cistercians, and others more strictly designated as monks, it would in some ways have been better to use the all-embracing title of "monastery" rather than that of "abbey" which only applied to a minority of the religious houses of mediaeval England. Nunneries, of course, are included in this book, so too are the military orders. I have, moreover, thought it helpful to say more on friars and friaries than was done in the earlier editions. Though the friars could be classed neither as monks nor canons regular, and though they could claim, like John Wesley in his widespread preachings, that "the World was their parish", their organization and rules of life drew much from monastic precedents. In time, moreover, they developed an important conventual life in friaries whose architecture owed much to that of the monks.

I have not, however, brought secular colleges into this book, nor are mediaeval hospitals in any way covered. One must, however, remember that here too the influences of monastic worship and architecture were strong. The hospitals, moreover, were often staffed by men and women under a rule of life exactly or closely based on that of the canons regular of St Augustine. The "religious" life of mediaeval England had ramifications taking it well outside the establishments which could, in the strictest sense, be called abbeys or priories.

A real problem is that of the cathedral priories (Canterbury, Rochester, Winchester, Worcester, Coventry, Bath, Ely, Norwich, Durham, and Carlisle), of the monastic churches (Peterborough, Gloucester, Chester, Bristol, and Oxford) made cathedrals by Henry VIII and still keeping their cathedral status, and of the cathedrals of St Albans, Southwark and Brecon which were once monastic churches, and have become cathedrals within the last hundred years. These churches (except for Brecon) are fully described in *The Cathedrals of England*, first written by Harry Batsford and Charles Fry and revised by myself for a new edition of 1960. They therefore find a comparatively small place in this book, and their architecture is not covered by its illustrations. It would, however, be both pedantic and damaging to cut these monasteries out of the text, or to illustrate none of their domestic buildings. The cathedral priories, particularly such monasteries as Christ Church, Canterbury and Durham were among the most important, and observant, of the Benedictine houses; no study

6

of the monastic life of mediaeval England could be satisfactory without them. So too, for surviving Benedictine cloisters and refectories one visits Gloucester, Chester, or Worcester, not Tewkesbury, Selby, or Great Malvern where the churches survive and are not cathedrals. Nor can any parish church which was once that of an abbey or priory rival Bristol Cathedral in the matter of abbots' effigies.

My last words of explanation concern the years after 1540. I have written a final chapter which deals with the antecedents of the Suppression and with its actual process, and which makes it clear that the religious life did not end among English men and English women with the suppressions carried out under Henry VIII and Elizabeth I. Both Anglicanism and Roman Catholicism have made their modern contribution to our subject, and, though few of the buildings so erected fall into the category of ancient or "historic" architecture, there are many modern convents of some architectural note. The whole subject of the monastic life is more familiar, and less controversial, than it was in the days of "Papal Agression", "Puseyite nunneries", or "Father Ignatius". One cannot rightly disregard the modern subject at a time when a Mirfield father has recently been a stimulating figure in England's religious and political life, when a Benedictine abbot is a familiar "personality" on sound radio and television, and when the great church in which that same abbot presides can be described by Professor Pevsner as "the most splendid demonstration of the renaissance of Roman Catholicism in England".

B.D.G.L.
Bristol, August, 1961

7

Acknowledgment

The publishers wish to thank the following for permission to reproduce the illustrations included in this book: Aerofilms Limited for Fig. 22; British Insulated Callender's Cables Ltd. for Fig. 27; L. Bruce Mayne for Fig. 8; C & E Photography, Bristol for Fig. 39; J. Allan Cash, F.R.P.S. for fig. 35; the late Brian Clayton for figs. 4, 5, 13, 14, 18, 32, 34, and 37; the late F. H. Crossley for figs. 9, 12 and 26; Leonard and Marjorie Gayton for figs. 2, 21 and 30; A. F. Kersting, F.R.P.S., for figs. 1, 3, 6, 15, 16, 19, 24, 28, 39, 40, 41 and 43; A. D. D. McCallum for fig. 38; Dr. J. K. St Joseph (Crown Copyright Reserved) for figs. 10 and 31; Edwin Smith for figs. 17, 20 and 33; the late Rev. F. Sumner for fig. 23; Reece Winstone, A.R.P.S. for figs. 7, 11, 25, and 36.

Contents

List of Illustrations

The photograph on the cover of the book, showing the choir of Rievaulx Abbey, Yorkshire, is reproduced by permission of the British Travel and Holidays Association.

1

Monasticism and the Orders

THE advent of monasticism, in the centuries of early Christendom which saw the breakdown and collapse of the Roman Empire, was largely caused by the manifold needs of the age. Cruelty, savagery, and the collapse of civilized life had become prevalent in many areas, and, though the beginnings of Christian monachism lay before the end of the Empire, there was now, more than ever, a need to find places where God could be worshipped with some degree of quiet and safety, places of contemplation and serious work in an anarchic world. The monastic system pioneered by St Benedict in the sixth century, and gradually developed into the monasticism familiar throughout most of the Middle Ages, was only attained after experience gained in various ascetic systems. First of all, in the deserts of Egypt and elsewhere, the hermits (whose title came from the Greek word for a "desert dweller") lived as solitaries in caves or tents. In some cases those with a prophetic gift would attract followers, as St John the Baptist had done, who hung on their words.

After the period of the solitaries there came a phase when hermits would gather together in groups. Next, those with a bent towards the religious life would gather into companies. These would often be of both sexes, and like the Shakers of nineteenth-century America they would have all things in common. They would follow no particular or rigid rule, but they produced early bishops and missionaries who did great work in the christianizing, or re-christianizing, of the countries of western Europe. In Britain many of the traditions of these early communities came from Ireland, and can be traced back to the ancient British church. Their members rechrisitianized large areas of this country, particularly in the North and West, and among them were outstanding men like St Patrick, St Columba, St Cuthbert, and St Chad. Their communities reached as far south as Glastonbury, and much of their activity was before the year 597 which saw the coming of the Roman monk St Augustine and his companions, with their Italian background and outlook, and their rule of life largely moulded by the recent example of St Benedict.

Monasteries for the reception of both sexes existed, in early Saxon times, in various parts of the country; one of the best known was at Whitby under the rule of St Hilda. This was also the period of the missionary *monasteria* – groups of priests in their life more similar to secular canons than to monks. Each one of these *monasteria*, or "ministers", would be responsible for missionary work over a wide area. Dependent churches would be founded to serve the needs of the early converts, and many of these would eventually become the churches of fully organized and independent parishes. The heyday of these early religious communities, and of the early monasteries like those at Canterbury and Jarrow on a more recognizably Benedictine pattern, was in the period about A.D. 750–800. But one by one they saw their career interrupted, or wholly extinguished, by the Danish invasions and ravagings of the ninth century.

It seems certain that all organized monastic life had been obliterated in this country by the time of Alfred the Great and his immediate successors, and it was not for some decades more that conditions favoured the revival of properly organized monasticism.

It was about the middle of the tenth century that England again became sufficiently settled for a revival of monastic zeal. A better system than the previous somewhat loose arrangements was found in the Rule of St Benedict, as this had by now been modified and developed by various monastic pioneers on the Continent. The Benedictines were bound by three vows: to poverty, against the deceits of the world; to chastity, against the lusts of the flesh; to obedience, against the snares of the devil. As originally evolved, the Rule divided a monk's activities between liturgical devotion, spiritual reading and meditation, and manual labour. The last of these three had greatly diminished by the tenth century, and the chief duty of a Benedictine monk now lay in the recitation of the canonical hours and the celebration of daily masses and other services.

The re-establishment of monasticism in late Saxon England is specially associated with the name of St Dunstan, himself a monk and the abbot of Glastonbury before becoming a bishop, and ultimately archbishop of Canterbury. St Ethelwold of Abingdon (later bishop of Winchester) and St Oswald of Worcester were associated with St Dunstan in this vigorous movement. A general code (the *Regularis Concordia*) for the English Benedictine monasteries was laid down. Many of the great Benedictine abbeys which remained important till the sixteenth century were established before the Norman

Conquest, and as the monasteries were for a time the only really effective centres of religious life in England many bishoprics were filled by appointing monks. These bishops, and the abbots, inevitably found themselves playing an important part in political and social life. Learned activity was almost confined to the monasteries, and at this period there were no monasteries or nunneries except those which followed the Benedictine rule. But the individual monasteries remained independent, and were not governed under a single head.

With the Norman Conquest much reorganization took place. The abbey churches and their domestic buildings were all rebuilt on a far grander scale, and many new houses were founded, starting with Battle on the very site of the Conqueror's decisive victory. At the same time much land in England was given by the new feudal lords to religious houses back in Normandy or elsewhere in France; on some of these estates "alien priories", or small claustral establishments of monks from the Norman parent houses, were set up. These were never of great religious importance, but the total area of these foreign-owned estates was considerable.

From the end of the eleventh century, and well into the next, England saw the growth, side by side with the Benedictines, of many other houses representing the various movements towards reform and greater strictness in the religious life. An impetus came from the enthusiasm generated at the time of the first Crusade, and new abbeys were filled with men, from all classes of society, more quickly than they could be built. The Benedictines not being thought sufficiently strict, a new order of reformed Benedictines came into being. This was centred on the long famous and influential abbey of Cluny in Burgundy, all the Cluniac monasteries being largely subject to the mother house. This idea, though good in itself, led to some impoverishment among the dependent priories, the funds contributed by them being used for the aggrandizement of Cluny. Though the Cluniac reform represented a return to the earlier simplicity of the Rule, it rapidly grew into a great political power and lost some of its religious fervour. Life in the Cluniac houses laid great stress on elaborate and splendid liturgical observance. The churches of the order were apt to be even more magnificent than those of the older Benedictines, and the cloisters were adorned with rich and curious carvings.

Towards the end of the eleventh century certain monks broke away from the abbey of Molesme in Burgundy to follow a stricter rule. They found a fitting place in a wild wood at Citeaux and there built themselves a wooden monastery where other monks like-minded joined them. For a time the hardness of the rule frightened away recruits, and the settlement was threatened with extinction. Stephen Harding, an Englishman from Sherborne in Dorset, one of the original members, became the abbot and the real founder of the new order. Before his time, Citeaux was the poorest and simplest of monasteries; when he died it had become the head of a truly centralized order which became very powerful and spread, in the Crusading lands, beyond the ordinary geographical limits of Christendom. It was severe and puritanical in outlook, with great emphasis on austerity and simplicity in its churches and their furnishings. One of its greatest members, the famous St Bernard of Clairvaux, thundered his denunciations against the luxury, temporal possessions, and architectural elaborations of the other communities; to these tendencies the Cistercians of his time were a standing rebuke.

This ascetic and strict order was at once popular, and new houses spread very rapidly. When by 1152 they had, in all countries, reached a figure well over three hundred, the General Chapter thought it wise to forbid any further increase. In spite of this, new houses were still founded; in Britain this tendency was specially noticeable in Wales. The Cistercian houses in England and Wales eventually numbered seventy-six, with colonies in Scotland and Norway. A notable characteristic of the Cistercians was their inclusion, for manual and agricultural work, of many *conversi*, or lay brothers. In time, however, the Cistercians suffered from a deterioration of their ideals, their members gradually minimising their obligations and becoming more like the general run of the Benedictines, for the literal observance of whose rule they had originally striven.

The Carthusians were founded by St Bruno in 1084 at La Grande Chartreuse. Their houses were known as Charterhouses, and there were nine in England. St Bruno, shocked by the worldliness of the ecclesiastics of his time, was convinced that, if you left the world, you must leave it altogether and shut yourself up within four walls secure from temptation. His rule was a return to the anchorite ideal, each monk living to himself in a separate cell, cooking and eating alone, and rarely meeting his brethren except for certain services in the church, and then with his cowl drawn over his face. He led a life of isolation in the truest sense of the word, and devoted his life to prayer, meditation and digging in his little garden. Such a life of contemplative austerity was forbidding, and the Carthusians were the only monks who, materially speaking, served no useful purpose. They produced no characteristic works of literature or benevolence, founded no schools, and did not help in the development of agriculture, though their monasteries had endowed estates and the order included lay brethren to do the manual work. The infirmary was absent from their buildings. If a monk was sick he was attended in his cell and when he died he was buried in the garb in which he lived, coffinless in the garth. We shall see later how the distinctive nature of the Carthusian life produced monastic buildings unlike those of all the other bodies of religious. The Carthusians never modified the strictness of their life and observance, and they thus retained the admiration of all classes of the people. Many prosperous merchants and members of the aristocracy were their benefactors, and it is worth noting that most of the Carthusian priories, including the London Charterhouse, Mount Grace in Yorkshire, and Henry V's royal foundation at Sheen, were started after the middle of the fourteenth century, at a time when no more new foundations, except those of the likewise strict Observant Friars, were being made of any other order. Several of the Carthusians, particularly the prior and several monks of the London Charterhouse, suffered martyrdom for their refusal to agree to the supremacy of Henry VIII in church matters.

Another order of extreme severity, but with its monks living a fully common life, was that of the Grammontines. There were only three of its priories in England, dependent on the mother house of Grandmont in central France, and with their small churches closely modelled on that at Grandmont. They deliberately chose wild and remote places for their priories, the best remains in England being those at Craswall, in a secluded valley in the Black Mountain country of Herefordshire, near the Welsh border.

In addition to the orders of monks there were also the canons. The secular canons do not concern us here, but the canons regular of St Augustine, from their habit called the Black Canons, lived together in essentially monastic communities under the Rule supposedly laid down by St Augustine of Hippo. This was more general in its terms than the more precise and detailed provisions of the Benedictine Rule, and being a more flexible document it was found to be of a wider application. It became the basis of the life of the Dominican friars, and was used by the brethren and sisters serving in many hospitals and almshouses. The Augustinian canons first came to England about the beginning of the twelfth century, were fairly popular, and spread with great speed. Eventually they had well over 200 houses, many of them very small; of the total about 170 remained at the time of the suppression. The average income of their houses was moderate, but they built some fine churches, of which that at Carlisle became a cathedral in 1133. Though they mostly lived in cloister like the monks, they were allowed, when necessary, to serve as parish priests (all of them being in priests' orders) in their appropriated churches. This happened with particular frequency in the early period of their history. Their monasteries were not under any central control, but like the Benedictines they periodically held General Chapters, and submitted to visitations by the bishops.

An order of canons regular, centred on a mother house at Prémontré in France, was that of the Premonstratensians, or White Canons from their habit. They were founded by St Norbert, followed the Rule of St Augustine (but in a spirit of more primitive strictness), and modelled their centralized constitution on that of the Cistercians. Prémontré remained the mother house, and was that where General Chapters were held. About thirty houses were founded in England. In 1512, owing to political and other difficulties, they were placed under the abbot of Welbeck who supervised them in the name of Prémontré. Like the Black Canons they would fairly often serve their appropriated churches, and like the Cistercians they chose secluded places for their abbeys and colonized them by sending out nuclei from existing houses.

A small body of religious whose life closely resembled that of the canons regular was that of the Bonshommes. They only had two houses in England, but the church of one of them, at Edington in Wiltshire, is intact and is one of the most beautiful small priory churches remaining anywhere in the country.

The Gilbertines were a purely English Order, founded about 1150 by St Gilbert of Sempringham in Lincolnshire. Their distinguishing feature was the revival of the double monastery, with a society of regular canons under the Rule of St Augustine ministering to the spiritual needs of nuns under that of St Benedict. There were also lay sisters, and lay brothers to do manual work.

During St Gilbert's life, thirteen houses were founded, containing seven hundred canons and fifteen hundred sisters; there were twenty-six monasteries of the order at the suppression. The rule described the construction of these double monasteries, which is here given in brief. "In the priory church a partition wall divided the church throughout its entire length, the northern and larger half to be used for the nuns. The wall high enough to prevent the canons and nuns seeing each other, but not so high that the nuns could not hear the mass said at the canons' altar. On the north side of the church was the nuns' cloister, and it was to be better built and more beautiful and more honourable than those of the canons. The nuns were to be closely guarded and the window at which they spoke to their relations was to be the length of a finger and hardly as wide as a thumb, and was protected by an iron plate. In the refectory of the men were two turn-table windows opening into the nuns' quarters, built so that they could not see each other; these were to be barely two feet high and wide. A high wall encircled the buildings."

Another "double" order of women and men was that of the Bridgettines, founded in the fourteenth century by St Bridget of Sweden. They only had one house in England, the royal foundation of Henry V, situated at Brentford and known as Syon Abbey. It was, however, large, important, and of great spiritual distinction right down to the suppression. Refounded by Mary I, it was suppressed again under in 1559. But its members made their way to the Continent and continued their religious life. Eventually the community came back to this country where they are now at South Brent in Devon – the only

English religious community of the Middle Ages to maintain its continuity to our own time.

Nearly all the other monastic orders had their houses of nuns, but only in the case of some of the Benedictine nunneries were these large or important. The finest church of nuns remaining is at Romsey, which was a house of the Benedictine Order, and the most extensive monastic buildings are at Lacock, a house of Augustinian canonesses.

There were two military orders, the Knights Hospitallers and the Templars. The former were founded in 1092 with the building of a hospital at Jerusalem, their object being to provide assistance to pilgrims visiting the Holy Land and to protect them on their way. They followed the rule of St Augustine and wore a black dress with a white cross upon it. They built their first house in England in 1100, and over fifty-three lesser houses were attached to it. They rose to great wealth and importance. Their head the Grand-Prior was the first baron of England and had a seat in the House of Lords. Guyot de Provens says of them, "I have lived with them at Jerusalem, and have seen them proud and fierce. Besides, since by name and foundation they ought to be hospitable, why are they not so in reality? A monk in vain leads a hard life, fasts, labours, chants, and reads the scriptures, if he is not charitable; it is only an uninhabited house, where the spider weaves his webs." The Templars, who were founded about 1118, were supposed to protect the Holy Places and to secure roads to Palestine. They built their churches in circular form in imitation of the Church of the Holy Sepulchre at Jerusalem; this point may still be seen in the restored Temple Church in London. They were rich and powerful, but being accused of various crimes they were suppressed in 1312 and most of their property was eventually handed to the Knights Hospitallers.

In the thirteenth century a new type of religious appeared in England in the form of the preaching friars. Their purpose in life was to reach the masses, especially the poor in the towns. The monks and canons had largely withdrawn from pastoral work, and many of the secular parish clergy were inadequate to the needs of the time. The friars like the monks professed poverty; they were not allowed to possess property, but received their incomes from alms and oblations. The churches and dwellings were generally held for them in trust, and they possessed no appropriated churches or presentations of livings. The various orders of friars came to England as follows: the Dominicans or Black Friars in 1221, the Franciscans or Grey Friars in 1224, the Carmelites or White Friars in 1238 and the Austin Friars a few years later. There were other orders, but the four enumerated were the principal ones. They were received with enthusiasm, to the annoyance of the regulars and secular priests, for they had the Pope's permission to preach and make collections in all parish churches, and were held in sufficient reverence by the people to make it a privilege for the nobles to be buried in their churches. They lived in convents, except those who had licence to travel unattached, and their houses were under the supervision of the heads of their various orders.

To aid their work of preaching and apologetics they encouraged theological studies and other learning, and soon established themselves at both Universities. Many of their houses, particularly those of the Dominicans, had their theological schools, and they had valuable libraries. They were much in demand as confessors and preachers at court, and many of their members rose to eminence. Robert Kilwardby, Archbishop of Canterbury from 1272 to 1279, was a Dominican, and his successor John Peckham was a Franciscan; so too were the scholars Roger Bacon and Duns Scotus. Hamo of Faversham was an early General of the entire Franciscan order, and the English Carmelites, among them St Simon Stock who was the Carmelites' General from 1247, were of particular importance in their order as a whole. Some houses of the Augustinians and Carmelites, including the Carmelite friary of Aylesford which has, in recent years, been reoccupied by members of the order, were in country districts. But most friaries were in the towns, where the friars laboured amidst squalor, poverty, disease, and vice. But the friars, like the monks and canons regular, tended in time to fall seriously below their earlier standards of zeal and devotion. The Observant Franciscans, a body of friars who aimed at a return to the original austerity of the Franciscan life, were therefore introduced into England late in the fifteenth century. Their friaries only numbered seven, but they remained strict in their orthodoxy and observance. They were among the sternest opponents of Henry VIII's divorce, and several of them were executed before the suppression. There were also a few houses of Dominican and Franciscan (Poor Clare) nuns, of late foundation and of high standards of observance and devotion.

Despite the maintenance in the monasteries of fairly large numbers of inmates the country was turning away from monasticism by the end of the Middle Ages. Except among the Carthusians, Bridgettines, and Observant friars (all of whom had attained maturity in the late mediaeval period), and in a few houses of the other orders, a sense of vocation and a desire to abide by the stricter spirit of the Rules had greatly lessened; for many, monasticism had become less a vocation than a secure and reasonably comfortable profession. The monks had become far richer, and socially more powerful than their founders had envisaged, and their houses, particularly the small establishments of the Black Canons, were far too numerous. In some houses there were serious conditions of bad conduct and irregularity. One may largely discount the politically inspired "revelations" of Henry VIII's Commissioners, but one feels that though not many of the monks and nuns were actually wicked they were very deficient when viewed against the original ideals of their orders. Earlier, the monasteries had filled the needs of their time, and during unsettled and disorderly periods they had materially helped in the development of learning, agriculture, and the arts. By now, however, the Universities had become the main intellectual centres of the country, and Colleges were being founded instead of new monasteries. Several years before the main catastrophe many religious houses (including, for reasons of international politics, the "alien priories") were suppressed and much of their property was given to new seats of learning, or else to other and more vigorous religious houses like Canterbury Cathedral Priory, Syon Abbey and some of the Carthusian priories.

2

The Convent: Organization and Personnel

ONE has, at the outset of this chapter, to bear in mind that there were in the Middle Ages many differences in organization as between the different orders, and between individual houses in each order. There were also many changes and developments during the six centuries between the days of St Dunstan and the suppression under Henry VIII. The organization of an abbey, like the spiritual conditions among its members, could be very different in the "monastic centuries" (i.e. the eleventh to the thirteenth) from what they were in the early Tudor decades. Again, the great variations in size, revenues, and numbers of inmates acted strongly against uniformity in internal arrangements. It is obvious, for instance, that the more elaborate divisions of responsibility, and the existence of numerous semi-independent "departments", would not occur in the numerous small and poorly endowed religious houses, particularly of the Black Canons, which were found alongside the large abbeys with their numerous monks and extensive estates. What follows in this chapter must thus, in the main, be taken as referring to the larger monasteries, chiefly Benedictine but in some cases Cistercian or Augustinian, and to the immediately post-Conquest period rather than to that when both numbers and observance had declined.

The head of a large Benedictine monastery was the

abbot, but, if the monastic church (as at Christ Church, Canterbury, Durham, and elsewhere) was a cathedral and contained a bishop's throne, the head of the convent was called the prior. In the Cistercian and Premonstratensian Orders he was always styled abbot, but in the houses of the Augustinian canons, except for some large ones like Osney or Cirencester, he was more often known as the prior. All priories, of whatever size, dependent on larger monasteries were called "cells", and their priors were elected by the mother house.

The more important conventual officers were known as Obedientiaries, and their departments were apt to be separately endowed and keep separate accounts. This financial system did not, however, prevail among the Cistercians, or among the Austin canons after 1220. It was open to serious abuses and caused inefficiency, so that attempts were in time made to bring all, or nearly all, a monastery's finances under the control of a single bursar or treasurer.

The chief officials, in a large convent, would be the precentor, sacrist, cellarer, infirmarian, chamberlain, almoner, hosteller or guestmaster, and sometimes the refectorian. Other minor officials were at all times without endowments of their own. In the following pages an attempt has been made, very largely by drawing on various ordinances and custumals whose text has survived, to give an account of the work of each officer. Because men are human the ideals therein set out were seldom fully attained, and the monastic chronicles are full of the mistakes and shortcomings of those placed in office. In a convent, where the selection was limited, men were sometimes given a position for which they were unfitted, the

monk's real character not being disclosed until power
was placed in his hands.

THE ABBOT

The head of the convent, whether he were an abbot or a
prior, was the absolute ruler; he was the father, treated
with the greatest reverence by his subordinates, and, with
few exceptions, could appoint or depose any official
under him. In the early days of the monastic ideal, he
ate and slept with the brethren, and was the example to
whom they looked for guidance in their own lives. There
is a sketch of Ailred, Abbot of Rievaulx, at the close of
the twelfth century, by his chronicler Walter Daniel. "In
his old age he had 740 men under him, and on great
festivals the church was so packed with the brethren as
to resemble a hive of bees. He was a mild disciplinarian,
and it says much for his character that life was as smooth
as it was. He was refined, courteous, gentle and firm almost to obstinacy. He was a man of pleasant and easy
speech, with a memory stored with anecdotes. He was
distinguished, industrious and physically frail. He had a
distressing malady and lived and slept in a little room
near the farmery, took hot baths, and as the end drew
nigh crouched over a fire. He would talk with his monks,
sometimes twenty together. He was friendly to the
younger monks, and one of them became the staff of his
old age."

This early patriarchal attitude of the abbot eventually
grew into something quite different. For this there were
many reasons, not all of them reflecting the decline in
vocational fervour which undoubtedly set in late in the
Middle Ages. From as far back as Saxon times, when

the monasteries had a virtual monopoly of education and of ecclesiastical talent, their greater abbots were inevitably drawn into public and political affairs; this continued with the evolution of the House of Lords (to which several of the leading abbots were summoned), and with the important place that great landlords like the heads of monasteries could not fail to hold in feudal and manorial society. It was thus impossible, even in the more austere orders and among the most conscientious heads of houses, for abbots to be invariably resident in their monasteries. But things were certainly carried much further in this direction than was really necessary. The abbot gradually withdrew into lodgings of his own which were quite separate from the rest of the buildings, and one even finds, at the small Cistercian abbey of Cleeve in Somerset, that the monks' refectory, as rebuilt in the fifteenth century, could also be used as the abbot's great hall for the entertainment of his guests. A great abbot became very much like any other important nobleman or landowner, travelling about with a train of attendants, including the sons of gentry sent to him for education and for service as pages; one even hears, in some cases, of the abbot's jester among his other minions! To such extremes did this go that Matthew Paris fulsomely praises Abbot William of St Albans because he attended the church services and chapter meetings and generally fulfilled his obligations of residence. On the other hand one knows of the "town houses" of leading abbots in such provincial centres as Exeter and Winchester, and early in the sixteenth century we find, from his revealing journal, that Prior William More of the Cathedral Priory of Worcester was hardly ever resident but spent nearly all his time at various pleasant country manors belonging to the monastery.

A monk's accession to the headship of a religious house could be by election by the convent or by appointment by the King or the Pope. An abbot was expected to be well educated, to have shown previous capacity for management, and to be skilled in legal affairs in case of litigation. As the Bury St Edmunds chronicler Jocelin remarks of Abbot Sampson of Bury, "he was thoroughly imbued with the liberal arts and divinity as befitted a man of learning, a literate man, educated in the schools and a master of them, known and approved in his own province". As in all autocratic governments, if the head was capable and conscientious, and devoted to his community, it prospered, but often the reverse was the case. The prelate might be saintly but incapable; or he might be positively corrupt. In 1191–1213, Roger Norrys was forced upon the convent of Evesham by Archbishop Baldwin. Norrys had helped the archbishop against the monks of Canterbury, and Baldwin rewarded him in this way. His abbacy proved disastrous, "for he wasted the revenues, using them in extravagance, and in support of his relations and others, allowing the buildings to decay, so that finally the brethren had to live on bread and water and beg for a living".

A despot could override all rules. No measure of scheming and economy by the obedientiaries could counterbalance a thoroughly bad head. The reverse occurred at Dover in the treatment of Richard Wenchepe, prior 1268–73. He was a quiet and inoffensive man who had done excellent work at Canterbury before his appointment to Dover. Following a dispute with the mother-house, involving a journey to Rome, he returned to find that the sub-prior had usurped his position and that the convent was in open mutiny. "Neglecting all rules and decency, the brethren locked the prior in his rooms for seven weeks, during which time the monks used his horses for rides to London and elsewhere, spending the revenues and scattering the property of the house". Eventually the prior escaped by night, trudging in the snow and mud eighteen miles to Canterbury in fear of molestation from the vagabonds infesting the roads.

THE PRIOR AND SUB-PRIOR

If the abbot was the head of the house, the prior was the second in command; if the prior was head, then the sub-prior came second. The prior was one of the officers whom the abbot could not depose without the consent of the convent. His position required tact and consideration, and it was essential for him to be in complete accord with his superior. His duties were to watch over the internal discipline and spiritual side of the convent. The Observances state "that he should be remarkable for his holiness, his charity should be overflowing, his sympathy should be abundant. He must be careful to extirpate evil tendencies, be unwearied in his duties and tender to those in trouble, and he should set before all the example of our Lord. His it was to admonish the rebellious, encourage the timid, sustain the weak, be long-suffering with all, and a true physician of souls". The ideal prior is indeed a beautiful character, but the human one generally fell far short of it. In the early days the prior, like the abbot, ate and slept with the brethren, but gradually came to have an establishment of his own, where he ate and there received his guests. After a time the prior's work in some of the largest houses was delegated to the second and third priors, and like the abbot the prior became a somewhat remote grandee, with considerable interests in the outside world. Unfortunately the abbot and prior were not always in accord. At Westminster Walter de Wenlock (d.1308) and his Prior Reginald de Haddam were estranged for many years, to the destruction of the convent's discipline and peace.

THE PRECENTOR AND SUCCENTOR

The precentor was one of the major officials of the convent. He was the chief singer, librarian and archivist, and organized the processions which formed an important feature of monastic ritual. The church services were under his management and were arranged by him. He picked out those who were to sing the lessons or responses, and "what he arranged to be sung had to be sung, and what he decided to be read had to be read". His place was on the right side of the choir, and that of his assistant, the succentor, on the left. He moved about the choir to regulate the singing and guard against mistakes. It was his duty to regulate the speed of the service; if the monks dragged, he must hasten them on. The precentor went over the lessons and matins with the younger monks and pointed out to them mistakes in pronunciation and time. In some convents he was the instructor in music, training the novices and teaching the cloister-boys to read. "He was on no account to slap their heads or pull their hair", this privilege being the right of the master of the boys. By the end of the monastic period it was not uncommon for lay choirmasters to be employed in some of the larger monasteries; we find the famous composers Fayrfax and Tallis in these posts at St Albans and Waltham respectively.

The precentor was the custodian of both the library and choir books, which he had to keep in repair and correct. The library was normally kept in an arched recess in one of the cloister walls close to the doorway into the church, the recess being lined with wood to keep out damp and insects. Sometimes, however, a separate room would serve as the library, as at Cleeve from the time of its first building, while separate library rooms became a feature of the larger monasteries and of friaries whose members concentrated on theology and other learned studies. The precentor catalogued the volumes and kept a tally of those lent out. If some neighbouring abbey or a noble household applied for the loan of a valuable book, permission was needed from the abbot, and its equivalent value required in exchange until it was returned. Many valuable books were the gift of the abbot, as at Croxden in 1303, when William of Evere, tenth abbot, enlarged the book-press and added many tomes. Transcriptions were made by the monks in the cloister, but no individual was supposed to write a volume for himself without permission. "If he showed pride about his work, he was to be punished by a course of bread the water." The precentor provided the parchment and pens, together with the ink, which was made from galls, gum, copperas and even beer. He kept the rolls of the abbey and also entered up the martyrology and the names of deceased members of the convent and their relatives. He prepared the mortuary roll, asking for prayers from other monasteries, and he was one of the three custodians of the convent seal and held one of the keys of the chest. The succentor looked after the lists and saw that everyone was in his place, and was to help anyone who could not find his place in the book. At the night office, "if he saw any one of the brethren drowsy, he was to remind him to be more alert as watchmen keeping their vigil in the Lord's service".

THE SACRIST AND HIS OFFICIALS

The responsibilities of the sacrist were many and important. He was responsible for the fabric and contents of the church, and for this reason, as one finds in particular with the Carthusian sacrists' cells, his sleeping quarters were as close as possible to the church itself. He had the care of the ornaments of gold and silver, vestments and furnishings, to keep them safe from thieves, clean and in good repair. The shrine was in his charge, and the sub-sacrist was often delegated to watch it at night. At St Edmundsbury in 1256 it was enacted that two persons should watch the body of St Edmund, and two others the church treasure and the clock by day and night, for in 1198 the watchers fell asleep, and one of the candles being insecurely fastened fell upon the carpets and the wooden platform before the shrine, setting the whole in a blaze, the church itself narrowly escaping. Among the duties which fell to the sacrist was the provision of live coals in iron dishes during the winter to warm the hands of those ministering at the altar. The sub-sacrist kept watch over the canonical hours, ringing the bells and regulating the clock. The sacrist provided lights for the church, refectory, abbot's hall, cellarium and guest-house. At Westminster the candles for the shrine and the royal tombs were a heavy item. For the tombs of Queen Eleanor, Richard II, Henry III, Henry V, and Henry VI over 1,434 pounds of wax were used. At the funeral of Henry V sixty torches each weighing fourteen and a half pounds were carried. The sacrist organized all the important funerals, the perquisites going into his funds; he also provided the obsequies of the brethren who died.

When the sacrist employed a plumber, mason, or any other workman he paid the wages, but the cellarer provided any necessary food. The sacrist was also responsible for various major building undertakings. So we find that Alan of Walsingham, sacrist of the cathedral priory at Ely, arranged for the building of the octagon and its great lantern after the fall of the central tower. The sacrist was not, of course, the *designer* of such works, but he was responsible for organizing and financing their erection. The office required a man of no ordinary intelligence, but that did not mean that it was always filled by such a person.

THE CELLARER

The cellarer, being largely in charge of a monastery's business affairs, was sometimes called the second father of the house, and he was certainly the Martha of his convent. His duties differed in different orders, but they were always important, and he often took second position to the head. In conjunction with the abbot, he managed the leases, buying and selling of land, appointing of overseers, and was often away visiting the granges and properties of the convent. The cellarer and the abbot seem to have acted on their own responsibility in the most important matters; and provided they were in agreement, they could do as they pleased with the estates belonging to the house. "For in matters temporal the cellarer is as it were the prelate's right hand. After the abbot he has the first voice in his own office, and all his servants should obey him as though he spoke with the prelate's lips". He was responsible for the mills, the malt-house, brew-house and the tolls and carriage of goods. It was his duty to find out whether the men on the granges and their foremen were industrious, or received tips, or stole; and sold the property of the house. He had the charge of everything concerning the food, drink and firing of the granaries. The cellarer's good management meant prosperity; but a house was not always fortunate in this regard. At Bury, Abbot Sampson found that the cellarer was always in debt, so he provided a lay clerk to help him with his accounts, to the indignation of the monks who considered it an insult for a layman to supervise the work of a religious. As time went on, however, it became normal in many monastic houses for laymen to be employed on clerical duties, while we shall see how laymen played a vital part in the supervision of monastic estates at a distance from the actual abbey. At the same time the cellarer himself, and sometimes also the head of house, had often to spend much time away from the convent on the management of its property, and many monks became highly expert as farmers and estate managers. The temptations of such a situation were considerable, and being much abroad was often found more interesting than the ordinary routine of the monastery.

The kitchener "had charge over all the things pertaining to the food to be cooked and served. He ought to be a truly religious man, just, upright, gentle, patient and trustworthy. He ought to know what food and how much should be set before the convent, with special commons for the sick. He ought to have the help of a trustworthy man to buy the food according to the different seasons, to lay in stores of provisions with judgment, and to avoid waste and superfluity. He should keep an accurate account, a sum of the cost each week, so that at the end of the month he can render his account to the prelate." He was to see that the larderer was properly supplied with meat and fish, fowls and other birds, and to be careful about the keys and allow no one to have them without his leave, and not put too much trust in cooks and servants on account of the danger of temptation. The kitchen utensils were to be cleaned every day and never taken away. "He ought to know the number of the dishes, and the cook ought to keep what is left after dinner until the kitchener comes in, and render each day an account of the dishes handed to him. He must be careful that food is not served in vessels that are broken or dirty, especially on the underside, so as to stain the tablecloths. Further, he is to be careful that no food is set before the convent imperfectly cooked, or putrid or stale; and no excessive noise or clattering is to take place in the kitchen. The cooks should have the food ready in good time, so that at the sound of the bell after service the convent can go straight into the frater, lest the brethren may have chance to grumble." The food bought for the kitchen of the small priory at Dover included "coddles, herring, whitynge, congers, hallybutt, muscelles, cockylles, mullettes, salt herrings, eeles, carpps, veal, sucking-pig, beef, pullets and vegetables".

THE FRATERER

His duties were in the frater, or refectory. He laid the tablecloths and had them washed and repaired, and provided new ones when necessary. He poured the beer into jugs, which were to be washed inside and out once a week. He was also to produce after dinner two jugs of beer for the convent and its guests, one freshly drawn, but the other filled with the liquor left from the other jugs. He washed the cups and spoons every day and kept a tally of them. He also fetched the bread from the cellar, and was not to offer it if it had been gnawed by mice. When the bread was laid on the tables it was to be properly covered up. The fraterer provided the mats and rushes to strew the floor and the alleyways of the cloister near the frater door. He was to clean the refectory thoroughly with besoms as often as this was required. In summer he threw flowers, mint and fennel into the air to make a sweet odour and he also provided fans. In winter he was to supply candles for the tables.

The fraterer also had charge of the *lavatorium* – the long, continuous trough, not far from the refectory door, in which the brethren washed their hands and faces before and after meals. He was to remove any dirt or dregs lying at the bottom of it so that they might always have clean water. He was to keep sand and a whetstone ready to clean and sharpen the knives, and to provide clean towels. The furniture of the refectory was simple, but at Westminster it possessed valuable plate, the gifts of the brethren and the King. The refectory at Durham was supplied with silver-plate, kept in an aumbry by the refectory door. "Every monk had his mazer severally to himself that he did drink in, and they were all largely and finely edged with silver about them and double gilt with gold."

THE CHAMBERLAIN

The chamberlain's office was domestic. With the exception of food, his department included all matters relating to the comfort and well-being of the convent. He and his assistant had the care of the dormitory. He provided straw for the mattresses once a year, when the opportunity was taken for a thorough cleaning. He was to provide warm water for shaving and soap for washing the heads of the brethren, also baths, for which he had to buy the wood for heating the water. Baths were taken three or four times a year, and he bought sweet hay to spread round the tubs for the brethren to stand on. Hot water was also required for feet-washing on Saturdays, and a good fire had to be kept in the calefactory. The heads of the monks were shaved every three weeks. They sat silently in two rows in the cloister facing each other; the elder monks were treated first, and by the time the water was cool and the towels wet the turn of the novices came.

One of the chamberlain's principal tasks was the provision of habits for the brethren. The tailory was under his charge, and he had to provide lay tailors who should neither be lightly engaged, nor lightly discharged. They had to know the exact shape and cut laid down for the brethren's woollens and linen garments, which must be "neither sumptuous nor sordid". At Barnwell every canon had an outfit once a year, but at Westminster the brethren were served in rotation. He also looked after the repairs; in one of the Custumals any monk who wanted a garment repaired placed it in the morning in one of the bays of the cloister, where it was collected and replaced when mended. He bought the cloth and skins required, either by interview or from the fairs. He was to find a laundress of good reputation and character to wash the linen, surplices, rochets, sheets, shirts and drawers; these were washed once a fortnight in summer and once in three weeks in winter. Great care was to be taken that no losses occurred and all articles were entered on tallies and returned in the same way. He looked after the boots and was supplied with pig's fat from the kitchen three times a year to make grease to keep the leather supple. The sub-chamberlain was to supply the lamps for the dormitory, to light them and extinguish them.

THE INFIRMARIAN

The Barnwell Observances state "that he who has the care of the sick ought to be gentle, good-tempered, kind, compassionate to the sick and willing to gratify their needs with affectionate sympathy. He ought to have a servant who is to stay continually in the farmery and wait on the sick with diligence in all gentleness. He should get their food ready at the proper time, and note how they ought to be dieted. He must endure without complaint the foulness of sick persons, and when they die get their bodies ready for burial. The master ought to say mass daily, and if they cannot attend chapel, go to their bedsides, repeating words of consolation, but not disturb them when resting. He should take a kindly interest in each one and should provide a fire should the weather require it, and a lamp to burn all night. He ought to consult the physician and provide them with baths, draughts, electuaries and all other things conducive to a speedy convalescence."

Many diseases were treated with baths, which were kept for the sick. In the larger monasteries there was a resident doctor and a physic garden where herbs were grown for the drug store. The infirmary was also the place where the eating of meat was allowed for reasons of health, though animal meat (as distinct from the flesh of birds) was not supposed to be served in the main refectory.

The infirmary was also used for the dwelling place of old and infirm monks who were no longer able to play their part in conventual life. They were sometimes allowed a private room to themselves. They were also allowed books, but these must be returned to the library and locked up at night. Conversation was allowed, and, as Jocelin of Brakelond says, "they told each other the secrets in their hearts". The infirmary was also used by those who were periodically bled, and during these "seyneys" they were allowed to spend two or three days there. The Cistercians, however, did not allow those who were bled into the infirmary, but they stayed in the dormitory.

Refractory monks were also sent to the infirmary, and there was sometimes a prison attached to it for such as had committed grave offences. It was also usual to send such monks to other houses for punishment and better discipline. Abbot Gregory of Whalley addressed a letter to the Abbot of Kirkstall, "Since the visitors decree that the bearer of this letter, one of our monks and a priest, is under punishment for conspiracy, and since he has for a year and more humbly and devotedly undergone the penance therefor; and as we cannot consistently with the peace of the brethren and the discipline of the order keep him any longer in our house, we beg you that you would keep him thus sent to you, with the right amount of clothing, amongst your brethren, treating him and causing him to be treated by others in the proper manner until we have licence to recall him. Let him be the last of the priests in the church, nor let him celebrate. Every Friday in Advent and Lent under penance of bread and water let him receive discipline in the chapter. I promise to repay you with a similar attention." Early in the fourteenth century one also finds that two canons from the notoriously ill-disciplined abbey of Wigmore were sent for the same reasons to the more observant Augustinian houses of St Augustine's, Bristol, and Keynsham. The abbots were unwilling to take in such undesirable guests, and episcopal pressure had to be used to get them to receive the disorderly canons for a time.

THE HOSTELLER

The monastery was often regarded in the Middle Ages as if it were an inn, with this difference that the guests were not obliged to pay for their entertainment. Full advantage was taken of this convenient fact, and the drain on the convent's finances at times reached breaking point, especially when the house stood near constant traffic, as at Dover and Birkenhead. The latter complained bitterly to Edward II over the ferry between Liverpool and Wirral, when people had to wait for days before they could cross; and the only habitation on the Wirral side was the priory. The house was so "often burdened with so many sojourners that it can no longer endure; the house has not sufficient for all the multitude of those passing and coming. They asked leave to build houses at the ferry and sell food to the passengers for the safety of the people and the relief of this poor house."

The Barnwell Observances give what should be the character of the hosteller: "As it is proper for him to converse with guests of different sexes and condition, it becomes him to have not merely facility of expression but elegant manners and a respectable bringing up. If he have no substance to bestow, he may at any rate exhibit a cheerful countenance and agreeable conversation. By showing cheerful hospitality to guests, the reputation of the monastery is increased, friendships multiplied, animosities blunted, God is honoured, charity increased and a plenteous reward in heaven is promised." It was the duty of the hosteller to see that perfect cleanliness and propriety were found in his department, clean clothes, clean towels, cups without flaws, spoons of silver, mattresses and blankets, and sheets not merely clean but untorn, quilts of full width and length and of a pleasing colour to the eye; in winter candles and candlesticks, a fire that does not smoke; writing materials; the whole guest-house kept clear of spiders' webs and dirt, and strewn with rushes underfoot. "He should have a faithful servant, who is not to go to bed until the guests have retired. He should be up early when the guests leave, to see that they do not forget a sword or a knife, and that the property of the convent is not accidentally taken away." Royalty lodged in monasteries whenever it suited its convenience, and even in towns where there were royal castles the kings sometimes found it more convenient and pleasant to lodge in local abbeys or priories. Some kings were generous with their offerings on these occasions, but others, like King John on a visit to Bury, were quite the reverse.

THE ALMONER

"Ought to be kind, compassionate and God-fearing. He ought to be discreet and careful in his apportionments, to endow with more copious largess pilgrims, palmers, chaplains, beggars and lepers. Old men decrepit, lame and blind or who are confined to their beds, he ought frequently to visit and give them suitable relief. He should submit to the loud-voiced importunities of the poor with calmness and ought not to strike or hurt or even abuse or upbraid anyone, but answer them with patience and moderation." His duties included the nomination of the poor men whose feet were washed on Thursdays, and the supervision of the letter carriers who took round lists of deceased religious for inclusion in the obit books of the monasteries of the same order. He and his assistant were to guard the cloister from intruders, to sweep and keep it clean, also the chambers of the sick, and to strew them with fresh hay and straw. He collected the fragments from the meals for distribution to the poor, together with the discarded clothing of the convent. At Westminster before Christmas he bought seventy-five measures of russet cloth to be divided up between twenty-five poor folk.

The children of the almonry and the song school were clothed and fed by the monastery. The song schools grew in importance as liturgical requirements, particularly those in connexion with choral masses and offices in the Lady Chapel, made for excessive increases in the choir duties of the monks themselves. The monastic schools were a frequent source of vocations to the religious life. The education of the boys in the song school was another of the monks' responsibilities, and in due course those not continuing as postulants or novices would be apprenticed to various trades. The convent kept a watchful eye on them, and visited them with gifts when sick. In the almoner's roll at Westminster in 1319 there is an item of 13s. 8d. "to keep little Nigel at school for a whole year for the love of God".

THE BAILIFF AND OTHER LAY OFFICERS

The administration of landed and other property was of great importance to a monastery, and there was sometimes a monk bailiff who acted as treasurer and kept accounts. He would also visit the manors and would sometimes hold customary courts there, together with the resident steward on the spot. But more and more it became normal for these duties, including the holding of courts in monastic boroughs and manors, to be done by lay officials, and the administration of monastic estates became an important activity for many laymen of the class of yeomen and small gentry. These men were also, in many cases, the tenants of the monasteries, with their families the eventual successors to the monastic estates. The senior officials would be the "Seneschals" – frequently members of the aristocracy who would not be called on to do much day to day supervision of a monastery's affairs, but who would be their "friends at court", and who would often hold several such posts in plurality, thus adding appreciably to their incomes. We shall also see how when the affairs of some monastery got into serious disorder they would often be temporarily managed by a committee of local gentry.

The property of Augustinian houses would often be cared for by a grainger and two receivers, while the houses of the Gilbertines would have faithful brothers as graingers. The lives of these graingers and manor bailiffs were not always easy. In the chronicles of Crowland concerning their church at Whaplode in 1481, it states that the parishioners were cutting down the abbot's trees in the churchyard. On hearing this he sent his bailiff, Alan Dawson, to forbid it. They replied, "What say you, monk? We shall that, and though the abbot himself were here continue to do so, and if he objected we should cut off his head." The Bailiff, alarmed, ran for safety to the church, the woodcutters after him with their axes. The enraged populace rushed on him, tore his cloak to pieces, nearly strangled him and took away his purse. The vicar, who was hearing confessions, rescued him, locking him in the vestry for safety. There they compelled him to write to the abbot, demanding his consent, or else send two sacks, one for the bailiff's head, the other for his body. The bailiff spent the night in the vicarage, the insurgents, armed with "jakkes, salettes" and weapons, surrounding the house for fear of his escape, others for the same reason sat up till midnight in the steeple to watch.

In the earlier periods, when the various rules were kept with the greatest strictness, and when a true sense of vocation was more likely to be found, the life of the regulars was one of considerable hardship. They were allowed no possessions; their clothes were provided for them, and when worn recalled and given away. They were not supposed to possess even a knife, a needle or a pen or writing tablets; they saw no money and were obedient in all things. They spent their time in innumerable services and study, living a dull existence in silence, shut away from the world and its excitement, for they lived on a low diet and suffered much from indigestion, a prey to habits which cut across the precepts of good health, and the constant and periodical bleedings were weakening. The average life of a monk was fifty-five years. The picture of a monk's life during an English winter is not to be envied. There was no heating in the monastery except in the parlour or *calefactorium* (it should, however be noted that the severe Carthusians had fireplaces in their cells). The dormitory, despite partitions between the cubicles, must have been icily cold when he rose for the long night service. He would then make his way, half asleep in the dark, to a freezing church, perhaps filled with a clinging fog, and was then expected to chant and pray with fervour for an hour and a half. One can understand the various unseemly incidents recorded, for human nature must often have been on the point of rebellion.

Archbishop Winchelsey's visitation of Dover Priory in 1299 is instructive on the conditions of a monastery at that time. Amongst other injunctions he says, "No

1 Tewkesbury Abbey, Gloucestershire (Benedictine): the Norman tower

2　Castle Acre Priory, Norfolk (Cluniac): the Norman west front

3　Bury St Edmund's Abbey, Suffolk (Benedictine): the fourteenth-century gateway

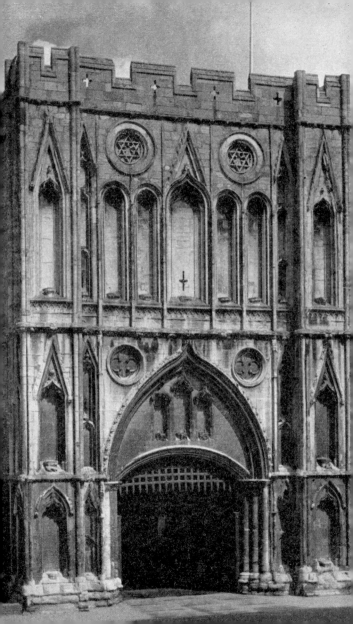

4 Romsey Abbey, Hampshire (Benedictine Nuns): the Norman interior

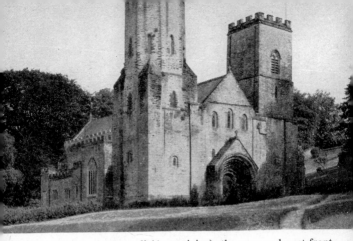

St Germans Priory, Cornwall (Augustinian): the nave and west front

Great Malvern Priory, Worcestershire (Benedictine): the church from the north-east

7 Gloucester Cathedral, originally St Peter's Abbey (Benedictine): th *lavatorium*, c. 1400

8 Haughmond Abbey, Shropshire (Augustinian): the chapter-hous arches, c. 1170

Valle Crucis Abbey, Denbighshire (Cistercian): the thirteenth-century chapter-house

10 Thetford Priory, Norfolk (Cluniac): aerial view of the ground plan showing church (*left*), cloisters (*centre*) and chapter-house (*right*)

monk must absent himself from the services unless sick. There shall be no excess of food or drink, that even the most captious can criticize. The strict rule of St Benedict is to be kept. As the convent is burdened with debt, let the brethren cut off all superfluities of food and drink and think only of the necessities of the poor. When not at services they must remain in cloister, and not stand about gossiping with new arrivals, asking for news and idling. As food is provided by the cellarer, so clothes are to be provided by the chamberlain, and for the future monks are not to be given money in lieu of garments or to expend it at their own discretion, lest it give rise to a notion of ownership or some other illegitimate desire. No funds earmarked for almsgiving should be used for paying the convent's debts. Since the dwellers in the cloister require quiet for prayer and study, all doors are to be closed and no layman permitted to cross it. No monk, official or other may lend or borrow money without permission of the prior, for the taint of ownership cannot but attach to a violation of this rule." But a visitation by Archbishop Warham in 1511 shows that by that time (as in many other monasteries) the Dover monks received pocket money or stipends. Individual monks would also come to own such things as pieces of silver plate.

THE NOVICES AND THEIR MASTER

The novicemaster was a senior monk, responsible and earnest. It was his duty to watch and teach the novices, and if any seemed to be of outstanding aptitude for learning he was to let the prior know so that they could be sent to the University. The novices were supposed to be at least seventeen years of age on their admission, the pre-Conquest practice of child oblation having ceased in the Norman period. Unsuitable persons might not be received, nor illegitimates without special permission. Until a novice was professed he was kept under severe discipline. The Barnwell Observances say "In selecting novices the brethren should be careful not to choose those whose election they may afterwards repent. They should ask as to their country, parentage, knowledge, behaviour, voice and power of singing, capacity of writing, and of executing any mechanical art; next as to their bodily stature, whether they possess everything they ought to possess, whether they have incurred obligations elsewhere or consort with any woman; whether they are in debt, if they have any secret malady, whether they are good-tempered, sociable, trustworthy and of good character, and finally if they are likely to be of use to the monastery."

Before he was clothed he had to confess his whole life to the superior of the house. He was then given a year's probation, and assigned for instruction a particular monk who was to teach him all the observances of the rule and the details of daily monastic life. At the end of the year he was asked if he could endure all aspects of the monastic life. If he replied in the affirmative he was professed; if not, he went back to the outside world.

In 1141, at the Cistercian abbey of Rievaulx, Ailred, afterwards abbot, was novicemaster. While holding the post he wrote a book in dialogue form, of which the following is a quotation. "The newcomer had been perplexed by the contrast between the spiritual rapture of the past and the aridity of the present. Ailred led him to analyse his early experiences. They had been delightful but passed as quickly as they came. He found equal pleasure in devout tears and in worldly jests. Now life was different; scanty food, rough dress, water from the well, a hard pallet. The bell rang just when sleep was sweetest. He had to toil and sweat for his daily bread, his conversation with his fellows was confined to a few necessary words with three people. He gladly agreed that this was only one side. Discipline meant peace; no wrangling or complaints of injustice, no law-suits, no respect to persons in high places, no favouritism in daily tasks. He was now a member of a community united by a common interest. Then Ailred brought him face to face with the issue. The conclusion was drawn: to love is one thing, to love with full surrender a harder thing. Love without service is like the emotion of the playgoers who weep at the sight of sufferings, which in the street they would pass unmoved. The novice hung his head. He remembered how he who had been so lightly moved to tears for his love of Christ, had been wont to cry with equal facility over the story of Arthur."

THE CONVERSI OR LAY BRETHREN

There were some of these in nearly all the orders. Their function was the performance of various manual work which was necessary for the running of the monastery or the exploitation of its estates. In the strictly contemplative houses of the Carthusians and Grammontines they took over a high proportion of the more "practical" work. They were of particular importance, and most numerous, in the Cistercian abbeys where they were at first indispensible for bringing land into cultivation and keeping it tilled; some of the more intelligent ones would actually be put in charge of outlying granges. In the Order's early period they were more numerous than the actual monks. At Rievaulx in Ailred's time there were 140 monks and 600 conversi. At Waverley in 1187 there were seventy monks and 120 conversi, and at Louth Park sixty-six and 150.

The conversi, being illiterate, were only taught the Paternoster, the Creed, and a few other elements of the monastic offices, these being said by heart and not read. They were not, therefore, admitted to the full habit.

The experiment of introducing a manual working element into monastic life was not an unqualified success, for the conversi sometimes turned out to be unruly, turbulent, and hard to manage, those who looked after farms appropriating the abbey's goods. At the East Yorkshire Cistercian house of Meaux in 1230 Abbot Richard Ottringham found it necessary to deal with the conversi in charge of granges, setting them to pig-feeding, ploughing, joinery, stone-cutting, and other work on the fabric of buildings. At Benedictine Evesham, between 1283 and 1316. Abbot Brockhampton found that certain brethren called conversi, whom his predecessor had placed in charge of the granges, had nearly demolished everything. They were recalled to perform their vows by fasting and prayer. At the Augustinian priory of Llanthony at Gloucester, it was laid down in 1250 "that the canons are to have control of the conversi both within and without the monastery, and that no conversus is to have any authority over the canons".

Difficulties over the control and discipline of conversi led to their decline, even in Cistercian abbeys, before the fourteenth century. It was found better and more profitable to let out land, or to work it with hired labour. This process was greatly accelerated by the Black Death and by the labour shortage which came as a result. As a result, conversi almost wholly disappeared, and in some Cistercian abbeys like Cleeve one sees how this development was reflected in the alterations made to domestic buildings. A few, however, were still to be found, and some of the conversi of the London Charterhouse suffered martyrdom under Henry VIII along with fully professed monks.

HIRED SERVANTS

From the first the monasteries employed hired servants, and eventually many houses indulged in this practice to extravagance so that they contained more servants than monks. At Durham in the sixteenth century there were over a hundred, and at Gloucester in 1380 there were 200 servants and officials to eighty monks. We have seen already how the abbots of the greater monasteries kept large numbers of servants, and many attempts to check this habit were unavailing. Much of the work which came to be done by lay servants was intended by the founders to be done by monks, but with the great growth of liturgical activity, studies, and work in administration this ideal was eventually abandoned.

The refectorian, chamberlain, almoner, and infirmarian all had lay servants to help them, and the cellarer had several, the most important being the caterer who helped the kitchener. The abbot's personal cook also had an important position. The larderer had charge of the keys of the outhouses attached to the larder, of the hayhouse, the stockfish house, and the pudding house. There were many cooks in the house besides the head cook and his assistants, those of the infirmary and guest house, the fish cook, the pittance cook, the salter and bakers.

Many of these posts were hereditary possessions handed down from father to son. In some cases they were bought, as at Eynsham, where in 1280 John Ireton was appointed for life as head porter, with various allowances, for which he paid twenty pounds. At Dover the post of head porter was held for two generations by Valentin and Nicholas Bere, and included a corrody.

OTHER INHABITANTS

Other people would sometimes live in a monastery besides monks, canons, and their lay servants. Convents were in the habit of granting corrodies to persons who had benefited the house by gifts, land, influence or faithful service. The granting of a corrody came also as an expedient to help the funds when they were low. It was a method of insurance on the part of the holder, and of speculation on the part of the convent, but in the long run it did the finances of the abbey more harm than good. An abbot wishing to raise funds could sell a number of corrodies to obtain ready money, the convent having in the end to repay or buy them back. The receiver of a corrody was often allowed to have a room in the monastery with liberty of movement. There were two kinds granted, one in which the recipient obtained the same food as the monks, the other being provided from the servants' hall. The Prior of Worcester granted to Richard de la Lynde, clerk, in 1308 "for as long as he lives, a room in the priory, with sufficient straw and firewood to be used when necessary in the fireplace; six pounds of candles of Paris tallow; twenty shillings a year of lawful money to be paid by the cellarer at Michaelmas. Every day of his life he will have one monk's loaf, one larger servant's loaf for his attendant, two gallons of superior beer, and one of servant's beer. Every day he will have pottage in quantity as a monk, and l.e will receive from the kitchen one dish of meat as a monk does, either cooked or raw as he prefers. For supper he will receive at the hatch allowance for two monks. He will have a stable near his room, with three cart-loads of hay, ten quarters of oats, also sixteen horse-shoes and nails." This was for money lent to the priory; others would be for various services rendered, as for physicians, musicians, and craftsmen. There were other corrodies which were wholly harmful to the monastery, as patrons would retain the right to pension off their old retainers on their foundation. Royalty formed no exception to the rule. Dover Priory suffered in this way from the patronage of Edward III, for as soon as he came to the throne he installed John Pyk, yeoman of the King's buttery, while in 1374 he pensioned off William Gardrobier, another old retainer. The same monarch, in 1334, sent Matilda de Plumpton, who had just finished her duties as the future Black Prince's nurse, to reside within the precincts of St Augustine's Abbey, Bristol.

Other persons, though not living within the monastery, enjoyed its protection. Apart from those, like Queen Elizabeth Woodville at Westminster in 1483, who sought temporary sanctuary in periods of political crisis, there were the permanent sanctuary men. Many abbeys enjoyed that right, one of particular note being the royal foundation of Beaulieu, to which Perkin Warbeck fled after the collapse of his rebellion in 1497. We gather, from correspondence dating from the time of the suppression, that several families then lived under its protection. We hear "that there are here sanctuary men for debt, felony and murder, thirty-two of them, many aged, some very sick; they have all of them wives and children and dwelling-houses and ground whereby they live. They have lamentably declared that, if they are sent away, they shall be utterly undone. We have certain knowledge that the greater numbers of them should be utterly cast away, their age and impotence and other things considered." The last abbot pleaded for them, and stated that they had been well behaved; it appears that most of the lay inhabitants of Beaulieu were sanctuary men and their families. The petitions were granted, so that they were allowed to continue at Beaulieu for life.

MONKS AT THE UNIVERSITIES

Apart from the monks resident in the actual monasteries there were, from the second half of the thirteenth century onwards, those who were studying theological and other subjects at the two Universities. The monastic orders were anxious to regain something of the intellectual primacy which they had lost to the schoolmen and the friars, so that they started sending their members to study in the Schools. From 1336 onwards they were supposed, under the terms of a Papal bull, to send at least one monk in twenty to a university, but this was found impossible by many of the smaller houses who could not spare their members on long absences from the choir and cloister. But many monks and canons

a
person
may go
to heaven

- without wealth
- without beauty
- without learning
- without fame
- without culture
- without friends

BUT NO ONE CAN
GO TO HEAVEN
WITHOUT CHRIST

For there is no other name
under heaven given among
men whereby we must be
saved. Acts 4:12

REPENT FROM YOUR SINS

Repent ye therefore, and be converted, that your sins may be blotted out. Acts 3:19

BELIEVE ON JESUS CHRIST

Believe on the Lord Jesus Christ, and thou shalt be saved, and thy house. Acts 16:31

CONFESS JESUS AS YOUR MASTER

If thou shalt confess with thy mouth the Lord Jesus, and shalt believe in thine heart that God hath raised him from the dead, thou shalt be saved. Romans 10:9

LIVE THE OBEDIENT LIFE

Not every one that saith unto me, Lord, Lord, shall enter into the kingdom of heaven; but he that doeth the will of my Father which is in heaven. Matthew 7:21

Silent Evangelist No. 253 (20¢ per doz.; $1.25 per 100)

SAMPLE PACKAGE ASSORTED TRACTS, $2

FAITH, PRAYER & TRACT LEAGUE
GRAND RAPIDS, MICHIGAN 49504-1390

(except from among the Premonstratensians) did in fact proceed to Oxford and Cambridge, and various methods were used for their accommodation. The monks of Ely had a hostel for their Cambridge students early in the fourteenth century, and we hear later, at the same university, of student monks living in such colleges as Gonville Hall or in secular lodgings where their lack of discipline and supervision gave cause for concern. In the meantime, the monastic Colleges of Gloucester Hall and Durham Hall had been founded for Benedictine students at Oxford, and these were followed by St Bernard's College for Cistercians and St Mary's for Austin canons. At Cambridge, Buckingham College was started in the fifteenth century for student monks from some of the Benedictine abbeys in the eastern counties. All these establishments were dissolved under Henry VIII, but fortunately some of them were soon continued under other auspices. At Oxford, important remains of Durham Hall, St Bernard's and Gloucester Hall are still to be seen in Trinity, St John's, and Worcester Colleges. Though the Gilbertine College of St Edmund's at Cambridge has wholly disappeared, all the buildings of Buckingham College completed by 1539 survive in the first court of Magdalene.

3

The Fabric of the Monastery

THE church, in the early days of some new foundations like Meaux or Fountains little more than a wooden chapel, was always the first part of the monastery to be reconstructed in stone. The easternmost part, including the monks' choir and the high altar, was built first, along with the eastern side of the claustral buildings which included the chapter-house and the dormitory.

The church was the centre round which the monastery grew up, and the building in which the main proportion of its inmates' waking hours was spent. It provided a fitting and adequate house where the worship of God could be carried out with dignity and ceremony. Its plan was a gradual development to meet the needs of the various rites which were added from time to time to the services of the church; such as the veneration of relics, the cult of the Virgin, and, as more monks became ordained, the provision of additional altars where they could each celebrate Mass. The finished plan also provided a suitable setting for the spectacular processions which formed a prominent feature of Sundays and Feast-days. Not all of these considerations applied, however, in the churches of the Carthusians or in those of many nunneries. The Carthusians said most of their daily offices in the privacy of their cells, and did not use their churches for processions. So their churches, except for the addition of some chapels for chantry and other purposes, were of modest size and of a simple rectangular plan which must have made their interiors resemble some of the simpler college chapels at Oxford and Cambridge. The nuns did not need the numerous altars required by communities of priests, so that their churches also were sometimes plainly rectangular in plan. In some cases, as in London at St Helen's Bishopsgate and at Wroxall, Warwickshire, a parochial aisle ran parallel to the nuns' church.

The cruciform plan, as evolved in the Norman Romanesque period with a long nave and a comparatively short eastern limb, provided accommodation for several distinct liturgical activities.* In the central crossing, or in the eastern bays of the structural nave, was the monks' choir, with a presbytery in the eastern limb for the high altar and ceremonies connected with it. The transepts were for communication and allowed space (usually in projecting chapels) for extra altars. The nave was for the use of lay brothers, servants, and in a good many cases for the laity of the adjacent parish. A Norman presbytery would be of no great length; it would be of two, three, or perhaps four bays and with its ending in an apse. It would usually be aisled on both sides. In some cases there would be apsidal aisles running parallel to the central presbytery. In other churches, as one still sees at Gloucester, Norwich, Tewkesbury, and St Bartholomew's, Smithfield, the aisle would be continued round the back of the central apse, thus forming a processional path, in some cases leading to a series of radiat-

---

* In a few small priories, like Flanesford in Herefordshire and Stavordale in Somerset, a monastic church had the simple "nave and chancel" plan of a parish or Friary church.

ing chapels. At Gloucester these chapels are arranged in three storeys – the lowermost in the crypt and the upper ones entered from the triforium. With the greater development of choral masses and offices in honour of the Virgin special chapels of great size were built in her honour. Some of these, according to the dictates of the site and other considerations, were built alongside the main body of the church, on the south at Waltham and Worksop, and on the north at Bristol, Ely, Peterborough, and Thetford. Eventually, however, they tended to be built at the east end beyond the presbytery. Many fine examples have been destroyed, as at Reading and Tewkesbury, but good examples remain at Winchester, Gloucester, and Christchurch. Owing to special circumstances one or two were built at the west end, as at Glastonbury and Durham.

With the Cistercians there was a return to the earlier English tradition of square-ended presbyteries; as their abbeys were all dedicated to the Virgin they did not require Lady Chapels. In many cases the eastern limbs were rebuilt or extended eastwards in one or other of the Gothic styles. These extensions were needed for various reasons, among them the bringing up of relics from the crypts and the erection of costly shrines for their reception. These were usually placed in a feretory which stood in the bay just behind the high altar; one sees this particularly well at St Alban's and Winchester, and this was the position of Becket's shrine in Canterbury Cathedral. These eastward extensions, as at Kirkham, Rievaulx, Selby and Worcester, sometimes made the eastern limb about as long as the nave, and in such cases the choir was sometimes placed entirely inside the eastern limb. This certainly happened at Canterbury and Selby, and in the latter case a new sacristy was built off the south aisle so as to be more convenient for the new arrangement of the eastern limb. At Bolton Priory the aisleless presbytery was extended eastwards in the fourteenth century so as to form a very beautiful un-aisled choir for the canons, the nave being walled off for parochial use (for which purpose it still remains) and the transepts and crossing becoming, as it were, an ante-chapel with subsidiary altars. The general effect must have been very much like that of such Oxford college chapels as Merton and New College, and from such late mediaeval alterations one sees how the architecture of the Oxford and Cambridge colleges was at least partly influenced by monastic examples.

As more altars were required, the processional path ran across the east end behind the high altar, and a series of chapels was placed against the east wall as at Abbey Dore and St Mary Overy, Southwark. At Foun-tains and Durham this arrangement was developed into an eastern transept of the full height of the church, thus forming a very fine architectural feature.

The monks' choir was separated from the nave by a double screen, having a central doorway with altars on either side of it on its western face. This screen was called the pulpitum; from it at stated times the epistle and gospel were read, and the organs were housed upon it. It was generally constructed of stone, and took up a complete bay, having within it a staircase to reach the platform, although there is a wooden pulpitum at Hex-ham. The sides of the choir were protected, for reasons both of draught exclusion and resonance, by parclose screens having doors on each side into the aisles, by the panelled backing of the stalls, and in some cases by solid stone walls which reinforced the feeling of enclosure and added to the resemblance between a monastic choir and an unaisled college chapel. This sense of enclosure is particularly well seen at Rochester, and in the choir and presbytery of Milton Abbey in Dorset. For in the latter church, whose eastern limb was newly built, after a fire in 1309, on part of the site of the abbey's Norman nave, two bays of the fourteenth-century eastern limb have stretches of solid wall instead of the open arches of normal arcades. The minimum space was thus left for access from the aisles and sacristy into the presbytery and choir. During the services the monks sat in wooden stalls, arranged "college-wise" on either side of the pulpitum doorway and along each side of the choir, the abbot sitting on the south side of the doorway and the prior on the north. Above the stalls, in the late Gothic period, were canopies to protect the heads of the brethren from the down draughts from the triforium and clerestory. These were designed from a simple covering to the wonderful spired canopies of the fourteenth and fifteenth centuries; unfortunately many sets were wantonly destroyed at the suppression. At Roche Abbey "the persons that cast the lead into fodders, plucked up all the seats in the choir, wherein the monks sat when they said service, which were like the seats in minsters, and burned them, and melted the lead wherewithal; although there was wood plenty within a flight shot of them, for the abbey stood amongst the woods and rocks of stone." In some cases, however, stalls from monastic churches were moved for use in local parish churches, as from Easby

Abbey to Richmond in Yorkshire and from Woodspring Priory near Weston-super-Mare to the church at Worle. In the middle of the choir stood a great lectern where monks "did sing their legends at matins and other times".

One transept frequently contained the night stairs from the dormitory, the best remaining examples being at St Augustine's, Bristol and Hexham. The transepts and their projecting chapels also provided additional space for altars. The first Cistercian transepts had a series of chapels, parted by solid walls and each with its individual stone vault, as one still sees them at Fountains, Kirkstall, and Buildwas. Later the transepts would be aisled in the ordinary way, the eastern chapels being separated by transverse arches and divided by parclose screens. The choir and transepts being private to the convent were shut away by screens, and as the choir extended one or two bays into the nave, these enclosed the eastern processional cloister doorway. The central screen, of which a stone example remains at St Albans and a wooden one at Dunstable, formed the rood-screen, over which the great Rood was either placed or hung. Unlike the pulpitum it had a central nave altar with doorways on either side. The bay between the two screens was used by the infirm monks, who could not stand through the long services. It is probable that the mediaeval bench preserved at Winchester was used for this purpose.

The nave was always the last portion to be erected, the process in some cases being so slow, as at Selby, Romsey, and Peterborough, that the style changed from Norman to early Gothic before the work was finished. In some cases the western part of a nave was at first parochial, but with the building and greater elaboration

63

of parish churches outside the abbey precincts the naves ceased to perform any very important function, so that they got comparatively little consideration during the various rebuildings and improvements which took place. At the time of the suppression the new church of Milton had never been given the nave planned for it, while at St Augustine's, Bristol the nave had either been demolished or had become derelict. The rebuilding of the cathedral priory at Bath, on a smaller scale than the Norman church and covering little more than the site of its nave, only allowed for a short and unimportant new nave, while in some other monastic churches, particularly those of the Premonstratensians, the naves were often long and aisleless or else little more than antechapels to the choirs. Monastic naves of other orders varied in planning. Some were aisleless, as at Lilleshall, and when aisles were added to such churches, as at Bolton, the side against which the cloisters were already built could not be used in this way, so that some naves had only one aisle. The naves of Cistercian churches were of extreme length in relation to the choirs and presbyteries and were used for the services of the conversi, low walls being built between the piers of the arcades, shutting away the aisles except in the western bay, which was always left open. When the conversi were dispersed, the intervening walls were removed and chapels and chantries introduced.

The nave would usually have a western portal used for special occasions and festal processions. Its absence is rare, but examples may be cited at Brinkburn, Buildwas, Cartmel, Furness, and Romsey. A further doorway, for the use of laymen, was provided near the west end on the side away from the cloister. This was often screened by a porch; an early, and particularly important, example remains at Malmesbury and there are later ones at Canterbury, Chester, Gloucester, and Great Malvern. In Augustinian and Benedictine churches the nave sometimes remained parochial and has survived, as at Nun Monkton, Elstow, and Dunstable, when almost everything else has been destroyed.

When the parishioners had the right to worship within a parish church, they were sometimes provided with a separate aisle, as at Romsey, Tewkesbury, Leominster, and Blyth. At Cartmel the south aisle of the choir was widened for their use. Two services in the one church at the same time could never have been satisfactory, and led to continual quarrels and unpleasantness. At Sherborne a parish church was built on to the west end of the monastic church. By keeping the font in the monastic nave the monks compelled the parishioners to be baptised by them, and an arch from the monastic to the parish church was constructed for this purpose; by lessening the arch to a doorway the monks incensed the populace, which led to the shooting of lighted arrows into the thatch which was protecting the rebuilding of the monks' church whereby it was burnt down. There was also trouble at Chester. The convent, wishing to enlarge the church, and the south transept being the only part available, they pulled down a parish church which stood in the way; the parishioners therefore claimed the right to worship in the new transept. This became so vexatious that the monks built them a new church without the precincts, which they refused to use, and they continued in the transept until well into the nineteenth century. During a quarrel at Wymondham a wall was erected upon the rood-screen, completely shutting off the nave, but the quarrel continued over the bells, the parishioners finally building their own steeple.

Towers played an important part in the general design of monastic churches. They varied in position and number, a single tower over the crossing, or two by the addition of one at the west end, or three, one central and two western. At first the central towers were low, as at Winchester and Romsey, and were surmounted by a pyramidal roof as at Boxgrove. Later, additional stories were added upon foundations not intended to receive them. This was the cause of so many downfalls and rebuildings. At the same time the danger of this expedient was sometimes realized, so that detached towers, in manner of the early sixteenth-century one still standing at Evesham, were built to accommodate the bells. Many western towers remain where central ones have been destroyed, as at Bourne, Bridlington, Worksop, and perhaps Christchurch. The Cistercians were at first forbidden towers, but as they relaxed their observance they too built them, as at Kirkstall. At Fountains, after vainly trying to build a central tower on inadequate foundations, Abbot Huby (1494–1526) erected a stately tower at the end of the north transept.

The churches of the friars, after very humble beginnings, attained considerable size and splendour, but were planned on much simpler lines than those of the monks and canons; only occasionally, as in the Dominican church at Gloucester, were they cruciform in plan. They were divided into two clearly distinct parts – an eastern choir, aisled or unaisled, for the friars resident in the convent and a nave for congregational preaching. These naves, mostly dating from the fourteenth or later centuries and some of them of great size, were very similar, with their central space and aisles, to those of large parish churches. A narrow, slender steeple, like that which is the attractive and sole surviving relic of the Franciscan church at King's Lynn, would sometimes rise above the central screen. The remains of friary churches in this country are unhappily scanty. The Dominican church at Norwich survives as St Andrew's Hall, and the Dominican choir at Brecon is still in use, as a school chapel. At Chichester the choir of the Franciscans is still standing, and at Gloucester there are substantial remains of the Dominican and Franciscan churches.

Although continual contemplation and the worship of God were the reasons for the existence of a monastery, lodging accommodation had to be provided for those who maintained the ordered worship of the monastic church. The domestic buildings were mostly ranged round the four sides of a more or less square garth or lawn, and between the ranges of buildings and that space where four alleyways, originally with a wooden pentice roof but sometimes later vaulted, in which the monks spent their waking hours, when not in church, eating, or attending to other affairs. At first the cloister, as it was termed, was unprotected from the weather, the walls being open colonnades looking upon the garth, as at Newminster. This in a warm climate such as Italy might be pleasant, but in England with its changeable climate and cold winters it proved altogether too austere for the brethren. and the cloister walls were eventually built in with a series of windows, as at Lacock and West-minster, which were glazed. They were also made more comfortable by the insertion of partitions or hangings to divide them into smaller sections. Even then, they remained unheated and were decidedly cold and draughty. Where the site allowed, they were usually placed south of the church to obtain the maximum sunshine and warmth. When this was impossible, especially where the town impinged on the monastery as at Gloucester and Canterbury, the cloister lay on the north side to be as far as possible from the noise. At Tintern, a northern plan was dictated by rising ground to the south and by the need for the most convenient outlet for the drainage system to the tidal waters of the Wye; the same considerations of drainage were decisive at Stavordale in Somerset.

The general planning of the claustral buildings was similar in the houses of most orders, though it might differ in certain details. The alley against the church was the one principally occupied by the brethren. Its outer wall, with its windows, was divided into carrels; each taking up the space of half a window. These were partitioned off by wainscoting, wherein was a desk for the books, enough space being left behind the carrels to form a corridor. Carrels can be seen at Gloucester where the stonework remains, and at Chester, where they have been reconstructed. Sometimes stone benching was provided against the wall of the church, and each end of the alley was enclosed by a wooden screen. The books, as we have seen already, were kept in a cupboard or separate room not far from this row of carrels.

On the east side of the cloister the first stretch of wall

was that of the south or north transept. Where the church was unaisled and where the garth was small, as at Bolton, the transept wall would account for a high proportion of the whole. Between the transept and the chapter-house was a frequent position for the slype, or passage eastwards to the monks' cemetery. It was also sometimes used as a common room, where rules of silence were relaxed, though this might also happen in a passageway through the western range, where brethren would be able to see visitors and traders. If the slype lay further south in this eastern claustral range, the space next the transept would be used as a sacristy, or divided between the sacristy and the treasury. At Durham, where the arrangements are anyhow unusual in that the dormitory range lay *west* of the cloisters, the treasury occupied a similar position, near the church, in the western range.

Of the buildings running off the eastern alleyway the most important was the chapter-house, as a rule with the dormitory running over it or its entrance vestibule. It was next in dignity to the church, and in early times was considered sufficiently sacred to be used as the burial place of the dignitaries of the house; sometimes the bodies of the brethren reposed there on their way to their last resting-place. In construction the chapter-house varied more than any other part of the monastery. It was either oblong, square, apsidal, polygonal, or designed as an aisled hall, the latter being a feature of Cistercian houses. If rectangular, it often projected east of the eastern range, but in Grammontine houses this projection was avoided by making it run lengthways to the cloister walk. Many of these chapter-houses are among the architectural gems of their period, and even in its present desolation the great apsidal chapter-house at Reading, once barrel-vaulted with a possible reference to Cluniac precedents, is highly impressive. Fine examples are at Bristol Cathedral (both the chapter-house and its vestibule), Chester, Hinton Charterhouse, the entrances to those at Furness and Haughmond, the pillared halls at Lacock and Valle Crucis, and the polygonal ones at Cockersand, Worcester, and Westminster. Many polygonal chapter-houses have been ruined, as at Dore, Bolton, Evesham, and Margam, but we can still study the polygonal type in full preservation in various secular cathedrals like Lincoln and Wells.

The dormitory was built over the eastern range and generally extended for its whole length. Between it and the transept was a vestibule, and from this descended the night stairs into the church. When the chapter-house took up the full height of the range, a passage to the stairs was often left; otherwise the day stairs were used. These were situated according to convenience. A fine fourteenth-century example remains at Chester. In small abbeys they were often cramped in an awkward way, as at Valle Crucis, where they are built into the side of the chapter-house wall. Circular stairs were also used, as at Chester and St Radegund's, Bradsole, where one is built in the south-west corner of the transept, serving as both day- and night-stairs.

Several dormitories retain their roofs and are now used for other purposes. Those at Durham and Westminster are libraries. Those at Cleeve and Valle Crucis were used by later inhabitants for domestic purposes; that at Forde now forms part of a private mansion, cut into smaller rooms. In early times the dormitory was open from end to end, the beds being ranged with their heads to the wall with a gangway down the centre. Later, partitions were used, either in the form of curtains or wainscoting, to give greater privacy.

Running out from the dormitory at right angles, and so placed as to be readily accessible to the main drainage system of the monastery, was another building known as the rere-dorter or *necessarium*, in other words the latrine block. It was a long, narrow building, with a row of seats against the wall, divided by partitions and each one with its own window. Beneath, walled in, was a drain with running water, artificially cut or else a natural stream diverted. The undercroft below the far end of the dormitory was used in various ways. A passage to the infirmary often ran through it, and the rest included the calefactory or warming room, where a fire was kept burning night and day from All Saints until Easter, being the only warmth kept for the monks, apart from those who were ill. It was customarily situated beneath the dormitory, even when in special cases the dormitory did not occupy its ordinary position. At Gloucester the dormitory was at right angles to the cloister owing to the cramped space, and at Durham it was finally placed over the western range. In both cases the warming room was beneath it. In Cistercian houses the warming room was apt to be placed next to the refectory, as at Fountains and Tintern.

The refectory flanked the alleyway opposite the church, except in Cistercian abbeys where it ran at right angles to the adjacent cloister range. It was often, as at Westminster and Gloucester, built on an undercroft which could be used for cellarage. Few refectories remain intact, those at Chester, Worcester, and Cleeve being exceptions, while at Beaulieu the refectory survives through being used as the parish church. The refectory was oblong and of considerable size, being entered through screens like the great hall of a manor house. There were hatches for passing food from the kitchens, and it had aumbries, or cupboards, for silver and linen. Its two outstanding features were the reader's pulpit, and a representation of the Rood or Christ in Glory on the end wall above the head of the presiding officer; remains of the second subject are seen at Worcester. The pulpit in the greater monasteries was built out from the wall on the south side, with stairs constructed in the thickness of the wall. The best examples are to be found at Beaulieu and Chester; at Shrewsbury the pulpit alone remains, all else being destroyed. Excellent ruined refectories remain at Rievaulx and Fountains.

The eating of meat (except the flesh of birds) in the refectory was forbidden, but as observance became less rigid those in poor health were allowed it, and various other brethren got special permission to eat it. This necessitated a special room. At first, the infirmary misericord was used, but later second dining rooms, or "misericords", were specially built. Indeed, as the numbers in the monasteries declined in the late mediaeval period, these smaller dining rooms were often those normally frequented, with the main refectories used only on feast days. One has to remember that in many details life in the monasteries, and the use of some of the buildings, changed considerably between Norman and Tudor times.

The kitchens were closely connected with the refectory,

and in Benedictine houses were built outside the cloister buildings. Two kitchens of the greater monasteries remain, one (the abbot's private kitchen) at Glastonbury, the other at Durham. They are square in plan with fireplaces at the angles, the arches supporting octagonal vaulted roofs and the smoke being taken by flues to a central louvre. At Haughmond, the large chimneys of the more ordinary type of kitchen remain. In addition to the fires there were also ovens, as well as copper cauldrons with fires beneath them, and chutes for the disposal of rubbish. In Cistercian houses the kitchen came within the cloister between the frater and the buildings connected with the conversi, so that meals could be served to both from the same place. At Fountains the fires were placed back to back in the centre of the room; a door into the cloister made it easy to obtain the provisions from the cellarer's checker. In Cistercian houses the brethren or the lay brothers originally did the cooking, so that the inclusion of the kitchen within the actual claustral buildings was no breach of enclosure.

We have seen how the *lavatorium*, for the washing of hands and faces, was near to the refectory; close to it, as one well sees at Gloucester, was the recess for the towels. Many *lavatoria* remain in more or less ruinous condition, as at Chester, Haughmond, Worcester, and Norwich. At times they were made into a distinct architectural feature, as at Gloucester, where the *lavatorium* projects into the cloister garth and runs parallel to the northern alleyway. At Much Wenlock, Durham, Canterbury, and St Nicholas' Priory at Exeter they were separate buildings, like conduit houses, placed in the garth; that at Canterbury remains and there are fragments of the one at Wenlock, which was of marble with carved panels.

The western range was usually on the side of the buildings nearest to the outer court. Most of its undercroft was divided into various domestic offices, the chief of these being the cellarer's checker together with the buttery. The upper floor was often assigned for use as the abbot's guest hall, the remainder of the superior's lodgings being at one end, or in a projecting wing. These arrangements are well seen at Watton, Castle Acre, Muchelney, and in the Benedictine nunnery of Polslo near Exeter. The Cistercian western range was at first devoted to the needs of the conversi. At Fountains the fine undercroft of twenty-two bays is double aisled. It was formerly divided by a slype near the kitchens, which formed the outer parlour and entrance from the cloister to the outer court. South of this was the frater of the conversi. On the north the sub-vault was divided into cellars for the cellarer's checker, which was entered from the outer court, over which ran a long wooden pentice. The upper storey formed the dormitory of the conversi, from which a night-stair led directly into the nave of the church, the day-stair being on the western side of the outer court. When the conversi were dispersed, these buildings were put to other uses, often as the abbots' lodgings.

Of the buildings outside the cloisters the most important was the infirmary. It was generally situated on the east side of the other buildings and was connected with them by a covered alleyway. The buildings included an infirmary hall, chapel, misericord, kitchen, and sometimes a separate small cloister as one sees at Gloucester. The main hall, like those of hospitals, was planned like a church, with arcades, aisles, and sometimes a clerestory, the "chancel" being the chapel at one end. The parish church at Ramsey is thought to have been the infirmary of the abbey, and at Ely the arcades of the infirmary hall are imbedded in some of the canons' houses. The beds were placed in the aisles with their heads to the wall. If no remains of fireplaces can be found it can be assumed that there was, as in the halls of early manor houses, a central fire, the smoke escaping through a louvre in the roof. In later times the aisles were divided into separate chambers, as is well seen at Tintern, and small rooms were sometimes built out from the sides of the hall. At Westminster, when the infirmary was rebuilt, the open hall was replaced by a series of small chambers round a little cloister, where the convalescent and decrepit monks could walk and sit. There were in the infirmary other occupants other than those actually sick – the old and infirm and, in Cistercian abbeys, monks professed for over fifty years. In the same abbeys there was a separate infirmary, placed in the outer court, for the conversi. The monastic infirmary had its own kitchen where the meat served in the misericord could be cooked.

The earlier ordinance that the abbot and prior should sleep in the dormitory was soon abandoned, and indeed this became inevitable on account of the manifold external activities and responsibilities of the heads of houses. A semblance of the rule was, however, maintained in some cases by building a corridor to connect the dormitory to the abbot's lodging. In time this was also given up, and a new house apart from the claustral buildings was sometimes erected. In Benedictine houses this was often placed against the west cloister, as at Chester,

Westminster, and at Gloucester where it was eventually superseded by an entirely separate building, whose site is now covered by the Victorian bishop's palace. The original abbot's house became that of the prior, and on the creation of the see of Gloucester was used as the deanery. At Furness the old farmery was reconditioned for the abbot's lodging, and examples may be found in almost any part of the monastic courtyard. As the abbots and priors, being local magnates and in some cases members of the House of Lords, entertained notable guests, larger halls and additional rooms had to be provided. A fine late fifteenth-century example of such an abbot's hall survives at Milton, while at Westminster the abbot's lodging surrounds a small courtyard with the dining-hall on the west, and the kitchen adjoining its southern end. On the north against the church are the Jerusalem and Jericho chambers, and the lodgings were continued between the western cloister and the courtyard.

In the outer court stood the guest house, the almonry, bakehouse, brewery, granary, workshops, and various other buildings essential for the economy of a great self-supporting establishment. Dovehouses would also be built, as a rule on rising ground some distance away from the main buildings. This can be seen at Abbotsbury, and at Bruton in Somerset the picturesque dovehouse is the most important building of that abbey still standing. Fish-ponds were also important for the regular and guaranteed supply of an important commodity, and at Meare near Glastonbury the fourteenth-century fish house was the residence and working headquarters, near the edge of a great expanse of water still undrained, of the official in charge of the abbey fisheries.

In the entertainment of guests, the same division seems to have been followed in all monasteries. The nobles were entertained by the abbot or prior, ordinary travellers by the hosteller in the guest-house, and the poor in the almonry. The two last-named buildings were close to the gatehouse. Not many now remain, but the guest-house of Dover priory is now used as the school chapel, whilst the fine Norman porch at Canterbury was once the entrance to the almonry. A rambling building said to have been the almonry, partly of stone and partly timber-framed, exists at Evesham.

The gatehouses of monasteries have often been preserved; in some cases, as at Montacute in Somerset and Kingswood in Gloucestershire, they are the only surviving relic of the buildings still left above ground.

An important abbey had more than one entrance and there was a second or inner gate when there were two courtyards. The early examples show but a single arch, but in later types a wicket or postern was added for foot-passengers. On one side was the porter's lodge and the upper storey was sometimes used as a chapel. Perhaps the finest example remains at Thornton, constructed of brick with stone quoins; this was military as well as domestic, with barbicans. Many others are imposing, as the gates at St Edmundsbury, Battle, St Osyths, Kirkham, and Worksop. They descended in the architectural scale to the timber and stone gateways at Wigmore and Bromfield.

The monasteries naturally possessed many buildings outside their actual walls. In 1213 the Cluniac Prior of Bermondsey founded a hospital for poor boys which was built against the outer walls of the courtyard. In 1331 the abbot of St Augustine, Canterbury, built a school without the gates for poor boys, and there were schools in the almonries at Durham, Barnwell and St Albans. Almhouses and lay infirmaries were general. At Glastonbury twelve poor women were maintained, at Durham four aged women, and at Reading thirteen poor persons were fed and clothed in almshouses. The *capella-extra-portas*, or chapel without the gate, was a customary feature. It was used by women and other layfolk who were not allowed within the precincts. The chapels at Merevale, Witham in Somerset, and Barnwell are still in use as parish churches; others remain at Coggeshall and Kirkstead. More normally, however, the needs of the laity living just outside the abbey precincts would be met by the building of an ordinary parish church. In many cases, as at Tavistock and Winchcombe, these churches remained in use after the destruction of the abbey. There were also chapels for pilgrims on the roads leading to monasteries with shrines; the beautiful little Slipper Chapel near Walsingham (now housing the Roman Catholic as distinct from the Anglican shrine of Our Lady of Walsingham) is the best surviving example. Hill-top chapels included that on Glastonbury Tor whose tower alone survives, and the structurally interesting St Catherine's chapel at Abbotsbury. Inns were also provided for pilgrims, as at Canterbury, and important buildings of this type remain in the New Inn at Gloucester and the George at Glastonbury.

There were many other buildings immediately connected with the management of an abbey's economy, but time and neglect have destroyed most of them. At Glastonbury, not far from the George Inn, is a stone building known as the Tribunal, where the abbot's court was held, and at Wilton near Salisbury the fourteenth-century abbess' court house is the sole remaining building of that important Benedictine nunnery. There are also many granges and manor houses, up and down the countryside, which were originally in monastic ownership, and their rebuilding and improvement, with a view to obtaining higher rentals, was an important aspect of monastic estate management, particularly in the late period; some would, of course, be used as country residences by abbots or priors. Near Chester is Saighton Grange, once owned by the abbey of Chester, and at Meare the manor house, of great importance as a specimen of fourteenth-century domestic architecture, was an outlying residence of the abbots of Glastonbury. There are also several barns belonging to monastic estates, either close to the abbey itself as at Glastonbury, Torre, Buckland, and Abbotsbury, or on outlying possessions as at Sturry near Canterbury, Ashleworth in Gloucestershire, Mid-Littleton in Worcestershire, Doulting and Pilton on Glastonbury territory in Somerset, or at Tisbury and Bradford-on-Avon to store the produce (particularly wool) of the widespread estates of the Benedictine abbess of Shaftesbury.

In considering these domestic buildings which were once in monastic ownership one has, however, to be on one's guard against false attributions. On the strength of traceried windows of unquestionably Gothic character the idea often grew up, in the late eighteenth and early nineteenth centuries, that many mediaeval manor houses which were never in ecclesiastical ownership must in fact have been religious establishments, or at all events the property of monks. One is therefore still told that some such buildings were abbeys or priories. But it was, and is, insufficiently realized that there were in the Middle Ages few differences between the windows in, say, the aisle of a church and those in the hall of a layman's manor house. There were, in addition, the numerous "abbeys", "priories", and "castles" which owed their origin to the revived romanticism of the late Georgian period. Many of these remain, their titles a pitfall for the unwary. The most famous of all was William Beckford's fantastic Fonthill "Abbey" in Wiltshire; the same tendency is well satirised by Jane Austen in her novel *Northanger Abbey*.

Many of the points outlined in this chapter did not apply to the Carthusian priories, though it has to be borne in mind that the austere Carthusians, like other orders except the mendicant Friars, depended for their income on landed endowments, and that these were of considerable extent and value, particularly those of Sheen. We have seen how Carthusian churches were of simple plan and modest dimensions, and in studying their domestic buildings we have to remember that a Carthusian monastery was not only a community, but also a gathering of hermits or anchorites, each living in his own cell. The only places in England where the Carthusian plan can be studied are at Mount Grace, and to a lesser extent at Hinton and in London. At Mount Grace the priory consisted of two courts, the large cloister garth being the northern one. It was surrounded on three sides by separate cells, each one a two-storeyed cottage with a workroom upstairs and the lower storey divided into a living room, a bedroom, and a study. As a monk took

1 Malmesbury Abbey, Wiltshire (Benedictine): the predominantly twelfth-century nave

12 Worksop Priory, Nottinghamshire (Augustinian): the north nave
arcade, late twelfth century

3 Glastonbury Abbey, Somerset (Benedictine): the late twelfth-century Lady Chapel

4 Buildwas Abbey, Shropshire (Cistercian): the ruined church of the late twelfth century

15 Temple Church, London (Templars): the interior, as now restored

THE MILITARY
ORDERS

16 St John's Clerkenwell, London (Knights Hospitaller): the crypt c. 1200

17 Romantic Ruin: Llanthony Priory, Monmouthshire (Augustinian)

18 Abbey Dore, Herefordshire: the presbytery

THE CISTERCIANS
THIRTEENTH
CENTURY

19 Rievaulx Abbey, Yorkshire: the eastern limb

20 Landscaped Ruination: Fountains Abbey, Yorkshire (Cistercian)

21 Boxgrove Priory, Sussex (Benedictine): the choir, *c.* 1200

most of his meals alone in his cell the food was passed in through a hatch, L-shaped so that the servitor from the kitchen and the monk could not see each other. Behind each cell was a small garden, and at the bottom of it a small privy connected to a continuous drain running outside the claustral buildings. Separating the two courts were the cells of the prior and sacrist, together with the chapter-house (as in London, next to the presbytery of the church) and the refectory for meals taken in common on festal days. Behind the chapter-house was the church, and beyond it the southern or outer court whose space included some cells added after the foundation of the priory. The rest of the court was occupied by storehouses, the guest house which was adapted as a private residence in 1654, and an attractive vaulted gateway.

4

Daily Life

As in the chapter which sets out to describe the organization and personnel of a monastery one must, when reading of the daily life of a mediaeval monk or nun, remember that there were many differences between individual houses, and between the heyday and the tail end of the monastic period. So this chapter, like the earlier one, must largely be taken as referring to the larger Benedictine, Cluniac, or Cistercian monasteries at the comparatively early period when fervour and observance were at their best. But at all periods the routine here outlined must have been considerably lessened or curtailed in the smaller houses, particularly in the "cells" or in the "alien priories" where the number of resident monks was always small. It was also much diminished in the establishments, whether of monks, canons, or nuns, where the inmates had shrunk, by the end of the monastic period, to less than half a dozen or even to as few as two or three, and where conventual life, in buildings planned for much larger communities, must have been a mere travesty of what the great monastic founders had in mind.

Although the hours of service and the type of work done differed little in the various orders, except for the Carthusians the life was in general common to all. A monk's year was divided into summer, winter and Lent, the first of these extending from Easter to the middle of September. His day was the natural day from sunrise to sunset, and consisted of twelve "hours" which varied in length according to the seasons. The "day" actually started at midnight when the first and longest service took place. From then onwards the sequence of events is clear enough, but Professor Knowles has pointed out that there is still some obscurity as to the exact time of the day at which the various monastic activities occurred. The sacrist and his assistants together with the sub-prior were up early to prepare the church and convent for this nightly vigil. Awakened by the sub-prior ringing the bell in the dormitory, the brethren crossed themselves, rose and put on the parts of their habits in which they had not slept, together with their night boots of soft leather, said their prayers, and waited seated upon their beds with their heads covered in their hoods, until one of the bells tolled softly. They then proceeded down into the choir, a junior carrying a lantern before them to show the way.

In the choir the juniors occupied the stalls nearest the altar, the seniors those farthest away. The abbot and prior stood without the door until all had passed in before them, and then gave the signal for the bell to cease. Their coming into the choir was signalized by all rising from their knees and returning their salutation, and at once they repeated the triple-prayer and the gradual psalms, at which every one had to be present. At the end, those officials who had other duties to perform might retire, and the second ringing of the bells announced the commencement of Matins. At the beginning of the lessons the appointed reader fetched a candle, mounted the lectern steps, and held it so that the light fell upon

the place of his reading, each lesson being read by a
different brother. On the feast of the twelve lessons the
preparations for the service were made during the sing
ing of the *Te Deum*, servants bringing in a portable lec
tern, others the cope and vestments of the colour of the
day, and the sacrist with great solemnity bringing the
gospels from the altar. He then conducted the priest to
the desk, vested him in his cope and pointed out the
place for him to read, while the servers brought in the
incense and lights. The priest then chanted the appointed
gospels and finished with the prayers for the day, the
bells being immediately rung for Lauds. During the in
terval the lantern over the great lectern was trimmed
the monks either remaining in their places or taking a
walk in the cloisters to restore circulation. When the
bell had ceased the second service commenced, and at
its conclusion between one and two o'clock the monks
returned in procession to the dormitory, led as before by
a junior with a lantern. They then had their second spell
of sleep. During these early services the sub-prior or cir
cator went round the church with a lantern to see that no
brother was overcome by drowsiness. If he found one he
placed the lantern before his eyes and shook him, return
ing to his own place. The brother had then to take up the
lantern, until he also found a brother in like condition
when the same thing was repeated. The church was dimly
lighted by a few candles, and, as the brethren had been
roused from their first sleep, drowsiness would be diffi
cult to resist.

At daybreak the monks were awakened by the ring
ing of a bell, and they were seated in choir before it
stopped. Prime was not a long service, and immediately

after it a great bell tolled for the lay servants' and work-people's mass in the nave. The brethren went into the cloister, washed themselves, and combed their hair. The priests then prepared to say their private masses; other monks took their books into the cloister, while the novices went to their appointed place to be taught. Before the next service, should it not be a fast day, the brethren were allowed some slight refreshment, called mixtum, consisting of a quarter of a pound of bread and a third of a pint of beer or wine, taken standing in the refectory. During this, the first bell was kept ringing for morning mass, known either as the Lady-Mass because it was celebrated in the Lady Chapel, or as chapter-Mass because it immediately preceded morning chapter. The monks assembled in cloister, and, as the second bell tolled, moved into the church in procession. The mass was said in a low audible voice with no particular ceremonial. On its conclusion the great bell rang for the daily chapter. During its ringing the brethren remained in their stalls, the officials consulting together in the private parlour over matters calling for notice, the custodian of the cloisters seeing that all the doors were locked so that no one could enter during chapter.

The junior monks went in first, and when all were assembled they stood and bowed as the abbot passed through. When all had taken their seats, a monk read out the martyrology for the day; the duty priest for the week (the hebdomadary) read some psalms and collects, followed by the portion of the Rule assigned for discussion that day, and by letters from outside on the deaths of any persons in whom the convent might be interested. The names of the monks responsible for various weekly duties were then read out. Next came a sermon, after which the novices, lay brothers, and visitors took their leave. The chapter then devoted itself to the correction of faults. First a brother could confess and ask for forgiveness; then the circator made his statement of what he had seen and heard whilst going the rounds of the house; finally the accusations made by one monk against another were heard. The accused was allowed to make no defence or excuses; but no brother was to accuse another on mere suspicion, only on what he had seen and heard. After the accusations the abbot pronounced his punishment, which sometimes took the form of corporal correction. If an accused monk was to be flogged, this was not to be done by his accuser, but only by his equal or superior. He was to kneel and modestly divest himself of his garments as far as his girdle, and he who flogged him was only to cease when the abbot bade him; he was then to help the brother to put on his clothes. It should be remembered that flogging was regarded, in the Middle Ages, both as a normal punishment and as a healthy means of self-discipline, both inside and outside the religious orders.

The convent then considered any temporal business that might call for decision, the sealing of charters, or the admission of novices. Should the chapter prove short the brethren had leave to talk in the cloister until the bell rang for Terce. In some monastic houses this time was spent in a different manner, a part of the cloister being set apart for the monks' parliament, the abbot or prior being ready to hear those who sought for guidance, or had business to transact with officials, also to discuss matters of policy or points of difficulty connected with the rule. In another part the senior monks met to hear a devotional reading and discuss it afterwards, and in the western alley the novices together with two or three seniors asked questions about the observances or cited perplexing passages for their interpretation, ordinary conversation not being allowed.

At the ringing of a bell all books were put away, and the brethren got ready for the next service which, if Terce had not already been said, was High Mass. On this occasion the stalls nearest the altar were occupied by the senior monks. Before the proper and ordinary of the Mass preparations were made for the blessing of holy water, and on Sundays and Festal days it was at this point that the procession round the church and cloister took place. After the blessing of the holy water before the high altar, two officiating priests and two other monks proceeded to take it round the buildings. One pair went through all the rooms surrounding the cloister sprinkling them and saying appropriate prayers; the other two went to the dormitory, doing the same to each bed in turn, returning through the farmery and sprinkling the sick and infirm. Meanwhile the Sunday procession passed through the choir parclose door on the farthest side from the cloister, entering the transept and sprinkling each altar while the brethren sang an anthem. It returned by the path round the east end, and down the choir aisle into the transept nearest the cloister, sprinkling every altar, and then passed through the eastern doorway into the cloister. First walked the bearer of the holy water, next the cross-bearer between two acolytes carrying lighted candles, followed by the sub-deacon carrying the gospels. The celebrant of the Mass came last in the liturgical procession and the rest of the convent, with the juniors at the head, followed at a slow pace, the abbot being last. Ordinarily the procession passed once round the cloister, re-entering the church by the western processional doorway, and if there were any chapels at the west end the altars were taken in turn, the procession re-forming and proceeding up the central aisle, making its final station on the stones set for the purpose in the pavement. The nave altar was then sprinkled and those of the surrounding chapels, the procession passing through the two doorways in the rood-screen, reuniting in the bay beyond and entering the choir through the door in the pulpitum.

At Easter, and on Ascension Day, Whitsunday, and the Assumption processions of great pomp took place. Any shrine or relics the abbey might possess were carried, along with banners and lights. All the brethren would be in copes, with the abbot (if entitled to wear them) in full pontificals, and the vergers carrying their maces. The route included a station in the cemetery. On Palm Sunday, as in other churches, the returning procession found the main door of the church fast shut; during the singing of the *Gloria, Laus, et Honor* the doors were thrown open and the monks entered the church, making a station before the Rood before passing into the choir.

Dinner followed Mass, the brethren coming out of the church in procession, first going to the *lavatorium* to wash their hands and faces, sharpen their knives, and brush their hair. If dinner was ready they went straight into the refectory, but if not they stood outside its doorway. As this was the first full meal of the day the brethren would be inclined to grumble and be impatient if it was unduly delayed. The superior and his guests sat at the east end on a raised dais under the great Rood, the brethren at tables ranged down the sides of the room with their backs to the wall, but at a sufficient distance to enable the servitors to pass behind them. During the meal conversation was forbidden, and from the refectory pulpit the monk appointed read suitable portions from the lives of the saints or other homilies in a slow distinct voice, repeating any passage he considered sufficiently important. Nothing very definite is said as to the quality of the meals provided. There were two courses; the dietary was to be always so plentiful and good as to do away with all excuses for dining at private houses or inns. The monks could ask for every sort of fish, vegetables, pastry, fruit, cheese, wine, water or milk. Spices, figs, ale and cakes were annually provided for Lent, and the never-failing pork-pies, capons, fig-tarts and blancmange of rice and almonds appeared at Festivals. Beer was the common drink of the convent, or it would not have been a hardship to be put on bread and water.

There were many directions as to behaviour in the refectory, "the brethren ought to eat what is set before them temperately, cleanly and cheerfully; they ought to speak sparingly, and not let their eyes wander. A monk was not to sit chin in hand, or spread his hands across his face; each brother should sit up straight and keep his arms off the table. He was not to wipe his teeth on the table-cloth, or cut or wipe the table-cloth with his knife. When soft fruit was served, it should be placed in bowls to prevent the table-cloths from being stained." Spoons were provided, the brethren using their own knives; forks being unknown, they used their hands. "Those who served the brethren ought not to rush about nor stand aimlessly in one place, nor gossip with the kitchen servers even about the dishes they received." Extra dishes or "pittances" were also given to the monks at stated times, but dining in the refectory became unpopular, because meat could not be served there.

The monks' first duty on coming from the refectory was to wash their hands and faces, waiting in the cloister till all had finished their meal; all then went into the church for Nones. In summer they later went up into the dormitory for their midday rest. When this was over, there was no service until evensong or Vespers. The brethren occupied themselves in various ways, transcribing books or reading. The novices were taught, and there was time for recreation. At Durham there was a green sward at the back of the house towards the water where the novices played bowls, the novicemaster being umpire, and in winter there was often a skittle alley. On the stone seats of some cloisters are still the markings for the game of checkers. The monks were allowed to walk in the garden for exercise, and in some convents they kept strange pets; at Winchester we read of apes, peacocks and bears and other creatures being bought, not for the brethren collectively, "but by divers brethren each man for himself". This was the only time of the day when the brethren could relax from their multifarious duties and services, but with the ringing of the bell for Vespers at six o'clock, and earlier in winter, all books were replaced and they took their places in the choir.

Vespers was sung with varied ceremony according to the Feast celebrated. If it was not a fast day the monks then went to supper in the refectory, the meal consisting of one good dish and one pittance or extra dish of fruit, nuts or cheese. After supper the monks went in to church for a short time, afterwards waiting in the cloister or the chapter-house according to the season in complete silence until collation. This consisted of a reading of no great length, after which the brethren might have a stoup of wine or beer in the refectory and wait for Compline, either in the cloister, or in the winter in the common-room. The bell then rang for this last service of the day.

It will have been noted that the sound of bells was rarely absent from the air, either the small bells of the dormitory, frater, chapter and church, or the greater bells of the tower. They seem to have punctuated every occasion throughout the day, and they must have given an air of animation both within and without the monastery.

The brethren then went to the dormitory in procession and were not allowed to leave it until Matins. Regulations followed them even there; they were forbidden to stand upright when they were getting into bed, but were told to "sit down first upon the bed and then turn their legs under the coverlet; they were to take off their shoes under the clothes and sleep in their shirt, drawers and gaiters. No one was to sit near a light in the dormitory neither were they to sing or read there, nor must they be allowed a candle. A brother might enter the dormitory during the day but ought not to linger unless he wished to change his sheets, and no strangers were to be admitted." Night did not exempt him from perpetual watchfulness. The circator took his lantern and carefully made a tour of the house. When he entered the farmery, if the inmates were in bed, he stood in the centre of the room and flashed his light round in a circle so that nothing might escape his notice. He then passed through the dormitory, going down the aisle flashing his light on each side of him for the same purpose. When his examination was ended he extinguished his lantern and retired for the night.

It will be noticed, from all these details of services and other activities, that the daily life of the monk was minutely directed, one day differing but little from another except for the special services and processions, and the variation between a fast day with only one meal, an ordinary day with two, and a feast day with extra allowances. Nearly every movement even of his body was regulated, and the least infringement of the endless ordinances and injunctions might be reported and punished. This continued from the day he was professed until he died or became too infirm to carry out the full requirements of the Rule. All this must have led to a numbing of the senses and to a feeling of monotony, particularly in the period when many of those entering the religious life had little real vocation for its deeper aspects. There were, of course, exceptions to this tendency, and a measure of relief and incentive came to those who had a chance to rise to positions of responsibility as obedientiaries.

5

Financial Administration

FOR the management and financing of a great monastery specially trained men were required. But unfortunately the selection of those holding the obedientiary posts was limited to the inmates, and although in time recourse was had to the employment of lay assistants much harm came from the fact that many of these monks had no capacity to administer large funds. Similarly the abbots, though sometimes specially chosen from outside the particular house concerned, often had insufficient experience to govern communities of their fellow men. It is not surprising therefore to find that many houses were mismanaged and deeply in debt, for the head had the power to do what seemed good in his own eyes. It was only when things became a hopeless tangle that interference came from without, either through the bishop, patron, king, or the General Chapter of the Order.

In the early days, when monastic estates were modest in size or simple in their organizational structure, or when the lands were cheaply cultivated by serfs or conversi, finance was a comparatively simple matter. But later, when properties were leased out, when the "commercial" aspect of estate management increased, when servants had to be paid, and when food and other goods had increasingly to be bought, the finances of the monastic communities became both complex and involved.

The system of more or less separate "departments", unknown in pre-Conquest or early Norman monasticism, increased from the twelfth century onwards, with eventual attempts to reduce it to reasonable proportions.

Monastic finance, like everything connected with the system, was thus of slow growth, and as time went on it was found impossible to alter it radically, though official visitors frequently tried to do so. We have seen how the Cistercian abbeys always had single bursars, but with the Benedictines the system of obedientiaries and their separate accounts varied a little in each house, but remained the same in its essentials. In some cases, particularly the better organized cathedral priories like that at Canterbury, a measure of control was eventually exercised by single treasurers, but in many abbeys the revenues were never audited as a whole, endowments and properties being given for specific purposes and apportioned to various obedientiaries, who thus came to have independent funds of their own. They might at times transfer money from one fund to another as a help in times of stress, but they looked askance at amalgamation or any attempts at control from above. In certain cases, as at Bury, the abbot also had his own revenue. Though the finances of a house were frequently managed with ability, an incompetent obedientiary or treasurer could fritter away a monastery's income, or an abbot could mortgage its estates, incurring debts far in excess of the annual revenue. An indebted house seemed to have a fatal, and usually disastrous, propensity for borrowing money from Jews or Italian financiers, and when the appropriation of another church was sought the reason given, unless it were some unforseen disaster like a fire, was always

94

the poverty and financial disarray of the convent. Yet though houses often became deeply indebted, the chronicles show that under a wise abbot, like Sampson of Bury, a house could be freed from debt in a dozen years. The economy of the monasteries, being well rooted in the security of permanently held endowed estates, showed remarkable resilience despite frequent mismanagement.

An early reason for the subdivision of a monastery's funds was the need to keep some hold on the abbot, on whose character and ability so much depended. His position was unassailable, and although he was not supposed to interfere with the property without the consent of the chapter, he could always obtain his own wishes, and the convent would endure much before it would appeal for outside help. The brethren were trained to obedience and taught to reverence their head, and it required great courage to stand in his way or try to thwart his will. The system of having a despotic head had many advantages, but it left a monastery a prey to an astute or worldly man, who was sometimes imposed from without. Alternatively, a monastery might be the victim of an incompetent incumbent who, though spiritually minded was weak, and was importuned by his relatives for doles or positions. An abbot like Sampson of Bury could rule strictly, remodel his convent, replace inefficient obedientiaries, and fight the monastery's outside battles. But a man like Norrys of Evesham (who had eventually to be deposed) could lay his abbey waste and ruinous.

In 1375 the Abbot of Abingdon owed the convent £1,374, which by the end of 1375 was increased by £94; the whole sum had to be written off. In 1341 the Abbot of Lesnes in Kent was deposed by the bishop, who "judged him to be disobedient, rebellious and incorrigible, wasting the goods of the convent to the extent that the canons had not vestments to put on". The results of his extravagance fell upon his successor, for in 1354 a debt of £500 was due to the mayor of London, and the following year liabilities for £545 were admitted, both sums being twice the revenue of the house. In the thirteenth century the cathedral priory of Worcester had a heavy and growing debt, and money had to be found by borrowing, selling manorial crops in advance, and corrodies. In 1366, under the weak and incompetent Abbot Shillingford, the Augustinian abbey of Bristol had to be taken into the king's protection, and put under various local gentry as commissioners. This was because of the excessive sale of corrodies, the profitless leases of possessions, and excessive expenditure. Despite the measures taken by these commissioners to put things right for a time, the abbey was again in serious trouble, under the same abbot, in 1371. Another cause of insolvency could be dissension between an abbot and his convent.

It was difficult to depose an abbot. It could be done either by the visiting bishop, the head of the Order or the Pope. But this was often only the beginning of the trouble, for the deposed abbot could fight his claim from court to court and litigation was always costly. Should he win, as he sometimes did, life in the convent became more than uncomfortable. Even if unsuccessful, he might take reprisals, as at Lilleshall in 1331, and at Bindon a little earlier, when the deposed abbot attacked the house and carried away its property, or took possession of it with an armed force.

Mismanagement was not the only cause of indebtedness; the abuse of hospitality, especially by the nobles, officials and royalty, contributed to its cause. The successive taxes and loans imposed by the Pope and his legate, as well as the king's constant demands for supplies for his wars and expeditions – all these being special contributions in addition to the ordinary dues imposed on the realm in general – lessened the capacity of a monastery to continue solvent. Should the king's assent be required to the appointment of a new head, it was given only for a consideration in money. When a monastery was exempt from the bishop's jurisdiction, the Pope and Roman Curia compelled the prospective candidate to travel to Rome. He was there kept waiting for the confirmation of his appointment, and exorbitant charges were common. Building projects were also costly, and when carried out involved constant repair.

As is indicated by the Bristol scandals of 1366 and 1371, the procedure for helping a seriously indebted monastery could be as follows. An appeal would be made to the King for protection, especially against abuses of hospitality when powerful persons and their retinues demanded it and then long outstayed their welcome. In 1277 the King's steward was appointed to the poorly endowed Flaxley abbey in the Forest of Dean, on account of this Cistercian house's immense debts, "and no sheriff or other minister is to be lodged there or intermeddle therein without a special licence". In 1393 the rich abbey of Waltham, pointing out that "no lord or great person, except kings and queens, had been accustomed to lodge or stay there for any long time", got a royal grant that no such persons should in future lodge there without the abbot and convent's agreement. Bishops' officials were also apt to offend in this same way, for when consistory courts were held in neighbouring towns they would lodge for long spells, despite protests, in adjacent abbeys; the Archbishop of Canterbury found it necessary, in 1301, to prohibit such practices.

The men appointed to have the custody of an embarrassed abbey were generally local laymen of good social standing; they would often include men coming from the families who were the founders and patrons of the abbey concerned. They seem to have been selected in view of the particular needs of the case, such as lawyers, knights, and, if near the sea, military men, who by their position would give authority to the commission. The king's protection prevented proceedings being taken against them for immediate payment of debts, and they were granted either temporarily or permanently the revocation of corrodies and leases detrimental to the interests of the house. It was the duty of the custodians to see that a proper number of monks was maintained, that alms and donations were properly administered, "else the souls of the donors be imperilled". Expenses in servants and food were to be reduced, and the state kept by the abbot and prior brought down to a reasonable level. If necessary the abbot was to retire for the time being to one of the smaller establishments belonging to the abbey, all surplus funds being used for paying off the convent's debts.

The sources of monastic income may be divided into two – spiritualities and temporalities, the latter as a rule accounting for the larger sums. The first embraced patronage, appropriated churches, pensions, and oblations on the shrines and at the altars of the church. The second covered all other sources of income, whether from endowments or from sales of goods and produce. The oblations at shrines varied according to the popularity of the saint, the populace being additionally influenced by the degree to which the person concerned had been a rebel. St Thomas of Canterbury combined all the necessary qualities, and long remained the most popular English saint in the calendar. Canonization was not always necessary, and at Gloucester the immediate popularity of the murdered Edward II, whose body was buried in the abbey church, in part enabled the monks to refashion their presbytery and choir as a glorious chapel in his honour. It was thus desirable for a monastery or cathedral church to possess the relics of some saint, or some wonder-working image, for the benefit of its revenues. Such, the relics of saints apart, were the Holy Blood at Hayles, the Rood at Boxley, or the speaking crucifix at Meaux. The faithful, however, were fickle and, as in all mass movements, turned from one shrine to another. During the fifteenth century oblations at most shrines diminished, and by the sixteenth century had become a mere trickle where they had not actually ceased. The shrine of Our Lady at Walsingham was, however, an exception to this tendency, as we can see from the time when it was visited by Erasmus and many others.

Appropriated churches were the main regular source of income in spiritualities. When a church was appropriated the abbot or diocesan bishop was supposed, out of the income of the living, to provide a permanent vicar at a reasonable salary, but this was not always done. The whole system was wrong and led to the gravest abuse. Parliament endeavoured on several occasions to amend it, but with little result. A petition in 1432 stated, "that old men and women have died without confession or any of the sacraments of the dead, the children have died unbaptised because vicarages were left void for several years for the sake of gain". Some churches appropriated to houses of canons regular would be served by the canons themselves, particularly if they were close enough to the monastery for the canons serving them to return for the night.

The following examples show some of the abuses that could arise from this system of appropriation. In 1391 the priory of Lewes appropriated four churches and a chapel; thirty-five years later the parishioners complained "that the buildings had fallen into ruin, divine service was neglected, and hospitality withdrawn". The appropriation of a church included the fees for the sacraments; baptism, marriage, churching and burial. The last included according to custom the "seising" of the best horse, cow, silver and other goods belonging to the dead man. Pershore compelled the parishioners of their appropriated churches to bring their dead to the abbey. There the contributions due on a death were valued, half going to the abbey, the rest to the parish church. The body was then carried back to the parish church where mass was said, the oblations going to the vicar. The body was then buried in the abbey churchyard, the fees going to the abbey. In 1396 the abbey of Abingdon appealed on its right to force the parishioners of St Helen's to be buried in the cemetery of the monastic church, to legacies made to them on burial, and to all oblations arising from obits and anniversaries. The vicar and his parishioners had bought and consecrated a burial ground near their own church, and when the appeal was heard some sixty interments had already been made. The monastery won their suit and caused all the bodies to be exhumed, and the vicar and his parishioners were obliged to pay the costs of the suit and of the removal of the bodies to the abbey ground.

Temporalities included all other sources of income. They comprised the income arising from the lands given by founders, patrons, and others; manorial rights and dues; farming profits, and income from fisheries, woods, pastures, and minerals; leases, tenant services, and the work of villeins and serfs; mills and wharfage; judicial courts and their fees, wardships, and homages. Rents would sometimes he paid in kind, and in 1451 we find that Dame Agnes Banastre, the treasuress of the Benedictine priory of St Radegund at Cambridge, was receiving capons as well as cash from tenants in the nearby villages of Great Shelford and Coton.

There were also, in a more urban setting, the revenues from towns, including rents from house property and the tolls and dues from markets granted either by feudal lords or the king. At Westminster Henry III, wishing to add to the money available for building the eastern limb, gave the convent a fair for a fortnight, and compelled the citizens of London to close their shops and trade there, much to their indignation. At Chester, the abbey had a fair granted to them by Hugh Lupus, to be held outside the abbey gateway, including the right to set up booths and rent them out. Traders were forbidden for its duration to sell or buy within five miles of the city other than at the fair. At Bury the London merchants claimed exemption, and not obtaining it, kept away for two years, "to the detriment of the fair, and the loss of the sacrist". Dover had the right to three fairs a year, passage dues, tolls on the Saturday market, and a tenth of the herring fishery, with a toll of the sea and wreckage. As the towns grew in size the convents were compelled to meet the citizens half-way, and levied dues in the place of tolls, thereby freeing the trade in the towns.

Fisheries, owing to the position of fish in the monastic diet, were important, and nearly every abbey had its fishing rights. Chester had a toll-free boat on the Dee, fishing rights off Anglesey for a boat with ten nets, and the tithes of some of the best fisheries in the area. Vale Royal let their weirs at Warford on the Weaver for the payment in kind of forty-eight strikes of small eels, and twelve large eels annually.

Monasteries were also trading communities, with the direct sale of much produce not needed in the actual convent, or found at distances inconvenient for its transport to the cellarer. Quarries, being a manorial perquisite, were valuable sources of building stone; those at Doulting in Somerset were used for Wells Cathedral and other non-monastic churches and brought large sums to Glastonbury. Coalpits were also a source of income on some Glastonbury lands, and the cathedral priory of Durham had coalmines at Ferryhill and Gateshead, while its dependent priory of Finchale had a mine with a horse-driven pumping station. In the twelfth century St Bees and Byland mined for iron, while Kirkstead had four iron forges, two for smelting and two for working, with the right to dig for ore and take dead wood for fuel. Bolton priory had lead mines, while many houses had salt pans, particularly in Cheshire. In 1284 the Abbot of Vale Royal was allowed to take ferm in Mottram

Forest for glass-making, and in 1309 he complained that whereas the late King Edward I had granted him a quarry in Delamere Forest, along with other easements, for the making of glass he was now prevented from building a house owned by his predecessors. Monasteries had other trades in their hands. St Albans had a fulling mill, and compelled all weavers in the town to use it. Meaux had a tannery, and in 1238 Tewkesbury sold the king's household a tun of wine made from the monastic vineyards. Repton and Malvern had tile works. Many hundreds of tiles from the latter, including some with dates in the 1450s, are in the priory church and in parish churches all over the area of the Severn basin. They were made to stock designs, including the arms of various famous families, so that it does not follow that a church which still has such tiles had any connection with the family whose arms appear on its floor.

The principal commercial asset of the monasteries lay, however, in the sale of English wool which was famous throughout Europe. Nearly all monastic houses possessed flocks of sheep, and when in financial difficulties would often sell the wool for years in advance. The abbeys with estates on the Cotswolds and in other great sheep-farming areas were of particular note in this connexion. As early as the eighth century we hear of sheep-farming activities by the abbess of the early Saxon minster at Gloucester, and later in the Middle Ages Winchcombe was of special importance. The *Valor Ecclesiasticus* of 1535 gives precise details of the sheep kept on their downland pastures by some Dorset abbeys; Milton, for example, had 11,990 in all. Such details explain the particular size and splendour of the barns which such abbeys as Milton and Abbotsbury built close to their precincts, as much for use as wool warehouses as for the storage of tithes in kind and other agricultural goods.

A letter of Abbot Gregory of Whalley is worth quoting as showing the sale methods employed. "Whereby the abbey contracts to sell sixteen sacks of home-grown wool, without coth, gard, black, grey, putrid scab, torn-off skin, grease, clact, bard, or bad skin", for a certain sum of ready money, which the merchant would pay to their representative at Boston. The abbey undertook "to deliver the wool at their own expense and peril, well washed, dry, and free from faults, of proper weight, weighed according to the custom of the house, in two instalments, unless prevented by a war in England or violent confiscation by the king; under penalty of £10 sterling for every sack in default. If, however, the king seized the wool in the first year, the merchant was to have all the wool for three years at six and a half marks for every sack; if the king seized it the second year and not the first, then he was to have the wool for one year at the same rate."

In addition to routine expenditure there were other occasional charges to be met. These included taxation imposed by Pope and King, levies of various sorts and charges made for leave to carry on the affairs of a monastery, such as the dues for permission to elect the head of a house, or alter its financial system. With the commencement of a new reign the deeds of the abbey had to be proved, and there was continual litigation over the monastery's possessions. These various burdens often proved altogether too much for the revenues and were one of the main causes of its indebtedness. Official visitors, either the bishop or those appointed by the orders, came at intervals to examine the administration and conduct of a house. This was a wasteful charge, for the bishop travelled in state with a large retinue, and, apart from the fees due to him, both he and his company expected to be well entertained. In addition, the servants in the bishop's retinue expected tips. Moreover, a bishop was an awkward person to cross. The convent at Whalley had, with Papal permission, appropriated the local parish church during the bishop's imprisonment. On his release he took away the church and fined them 1,000 marks, to be paid at 200 marks a year. Evesham, when claiming exemption from the bishop's visitation said "they knew not the episcopal burdens. Not only once a year, but as often as he will, he visits the monasteries subjected to him. Not only the bishops, but even their archdeacons, officials and ministers are admitted to the great grievance of the house, and their horses are put to lodge until they are bettered by their stay there; even the rents are wont to be given to the clerks of the bishops, with other intolerable presents, all of which are to be borne at one time, and the neighbours yet more heavily." When Archbishop Winchelsey visited the cathedral priory of Worcester in 1301 he deposed the sub-prior, precentor, chamberlain, sacrist, third prior, and pittancer.

Many of the greater abbeys struggled to free themselves from episcopal control, but found in doing so that they had if anything worsened their position. When the abbot of an exempted house was elected, he was compelled to travel to Rome for confirmation, bearing not only the cost of the journey, but the many delays by the

Curia. In 1257 Simon de Luton, prior, was elected Abbot of Bury, for which he paid 2,000 marks. In 1279 John of Northwold paid 1,175 marks. We hear of two abbots of St Albans spending large sums in having their elections confirmed at the papal court, and these cases can be paralleled at Westminster and elsewhere.

The exactions of the Roman Curia did not stop at such expedients as these. During the opppressive days of Henry III there is a record of continual exactions and extortions, both by Pope and king, who when it suited their convenience combined together. It was said they resembled the wolf and the shepherd together harrying the fold, each trying all kinds of inducements and expedients for extracting money from the religious. In 1229 the Pope took tithe from the clergy, which was paid under threat of excommunication. This threat was used so often and for such material ends, that its terror must have been lessened by constant use. In 1240 the heads of all religious houses were summoned to London to meet the legate Otho. They in their turn formulated complaints against the king. Churches had been kept vacant, the rights and liberties of the clerics had been ignored and abused. Promises were made to them, but the money demanded from them was not forthcoming. The legate then sent letters requiring immediate payments of large sums for the proper support of his dignity in the country, at the same time offering to excuse those who had taken a crusading oath, on payment of fines which were to go into the papal coffers. In the late spring the heads of the Church were again summoned with an instant demand for huge sums to help in the war made by the Pope against the Emperor Frederick, which were refused. The abbots could ill spare the large sums extorted from them to be sent to Rome. Bury and Battle complained to the king, who handed them over to the legate, offering at the same time to provide a fitting prison for their reception, and it was only in this extremity that the majority gave in. During 1240, as the legate had failed in his purpose in full assembly, he attacked them in smaller numbers, starting in Berkshire. They again opposed his demands and replying to him said "that just as the Roman church had its patrimony, the administration of which belongs to the Lord Pope, so the English churches had theirs, which was not liable to pay tribute to the Roman church; and if all churches were under the care and guardianship of the Pope, they were not under his dominion, nor were they his property".

Then in 1254 the Pope gave the king a tenth of all ecclesiastical property, and the following year, when the legate Rustard was opposed by the clergy, he obtained letters in blank to send to any monastery he pleased. He ordered them to raise money by borrowing, either five, six, or seven hundred marks for the use of the Pope. In 1255 he summoned the heads to London and demanded so large a sum that had it been granted, the Church and kingdom would have been ruined. At their refusal the legate and the king were angered, for both the king and the Pope were deeply involved in the foolish claim to the crown of Sicily. In 1256 the king ordered the Abbot of Westminster to pay 1,705 marks, which the king owed to merchants in Siena, and at the same time Rustard claimed five years' tax on first-fruits. The Pope also insisted on the finding of 2,000 marks, from certain selected abbeys, to pay his creditors. The legate also demanded a year's wool crop from the Cistercians, but they, who had refused to give way in 1240, again declined.

In the fourteenth century there was little improvement. The monasteries were charged with the duty of collecting convocation grants, and they shared in the unpopularity arising from papal exactions. In 1331, for example, the abbot of Burton's servant was assaulted and robbed of £100 he had collected for the Pope. During the French and Scottish wars of this period the kings were unremitting in their endeavours to get assistance in goods and money. The Worcester *Liber Albus* records various demands. In 1310 Edward II asked for sixty quarters of wheat, forty of barley meal, twenty oxen, and a hundred sheep "to be delivered to our sheriff to be conveyed to Scotland ready for our arrival". He also demanded wagons and horses and money subsidies in the same connexion. Other more routine requests could have their lighter side, and showed how demands could at times be met by sly evasion. In 1332, for instance, the Cistercian abbot of Revesby in Lincolnshire was asked by the royal bureaucrats to send a strong horse to carry the Rolls of Chancery on some official journey. The abbot, however, sent an animal which was "insufficient and useless" on account of its weak limbs. It was returned to the abbot, who somehow excused himself from a renewed demand for a strong horse to carry the bulky documents.

In 1347, the year of the famous siege of Calais, the king issued a demand for money and wool, expected in all to realize £3,500, in addition to the sixteenth demanded the year before. He also tried other methods. He had twenty thousand sacks of wool sold to the farmers of the customs below the proper price. In return, the merchants were to pay sums, between April and Christmas, which much exceeded the sum paid by the government. Much of this loss to producers must have fallen on monasteries. It was all part of the price that ecclesiastical establishments had to pay for their inevitable involvement in the social and economic system of mediaeval England.

Historical events and political conditions had their repercussions on the fortunes of the monasteries. The Scottish wars involved many northern abbeys in disaster and pillage, their estates being laid when the buildings were not actually destroyed. The same reasons of political disturbance and border warfare caused similar trouble to many Welsh monasteries, particularly in the time of Owen Glendower early in the fifteenth century. Frequent disturbances in Ireland often made the Irish possessions of English abbeys cause more trouble than they were worth. In the fourteenth century the recurrences of the Black Death greatly affected the financial and economic system of many monasteries, and accentuated an existing tendency to lease out estates rather than work them direct. Tenements in the towns would temporarily remain unoccupied or fall into ruin, while many other sources of revenues such as mills, woods, and fisheries were diminished. Political disturbances and civil wars like the Wars of the Roses caused the loss of many estates, monasteries being involved in the fortunes of their patrons. Tutbury Priory, in 1321, was mixed up in the revolt of Thomas of Lancaster, who when fleeing from Edward II left his war chest behind. The priory was accused of its possession, and was harried till 1325 when the monks were exonerated. Five hundred years later, when workmen were clearing out the mill-race sixty yards below the bridge, they discovered hundreds of coins in gold and silver, English, Scottish and French, which at that late date cleared the monks.

6

Building Operations

IN the early years, inmates of the monasteries lent a helping hand in the erection of their future homes, and later on both monks and conversi built the first temporary quarters of the Cistercian houses. This practice was, however, soon abandoned, and the design and construction of monasteries, as of other important buildings, was placed entirely in professional lay hands; the whole subject of mediaeval building operations has in recent years been greatly illuminated by the researches of Mr L. F. Salzmann, Mr John Harvey and others. The assertions of various chronicles that bishops, abbots, priors and sacrists must be corrected in the light of Matthew Paris's statement, "that all works must be ascribed to the abbot out of respect to his office, for he who sanctions the performance of a thing by his authority, is really the person who does the thing". No doubt these officials had not only the ordering of the work, but gave their decision upon its size and the type of architecture desired, it often being stated that a building should be like one already erected, but better if possible. The funds passed through their hands, and the sacrist or a clerk was appointed to keep the accounts. With the actual setting out and construction, however, they had little or nothing to do. The period now under review extended over more than five hundred years, and during that time the building system changed, so that well before its close all work was placed in the hands of men of professional standing. Much evidence on what actually happened is available in various records such as fabric rolls, and the names of many designers and master masons, for the Gothic period though not, unfortunately, for the years of Norman expansion and rebuilding, are well known.

When a major building was to be erected the first step taken was to appoint a working architect, called the master-mason, who took charge of the design, construction, and management of the work. This was generally a well-paid position, and its perquisites included a house together with a fur robe and gloves; if the work was on a large and continuing scale the post was permanent with a pension attached.

The master-mason had an assistant, but remained solely responsible for the engagement of masons and unskilled workers under him. Owing to the scattered nature of their employment, the masons were more or less nomadic in their habits, and seem to have had permission to travel from place to place. They moved about in small gangs, possibly owing to the perils of the road, and some of them owned horses and carts, which suggests their methods of travel. If they brought their own tools, these were bought from them when they started work and sold back when they left.

There were various grades of masons, paid according to their ability. The highest class was that of the freemasons, who worked the fine-grained freestones with chisel and mallet, cut the tracery, moulded the arches and capitals, and executed much of the carving. They

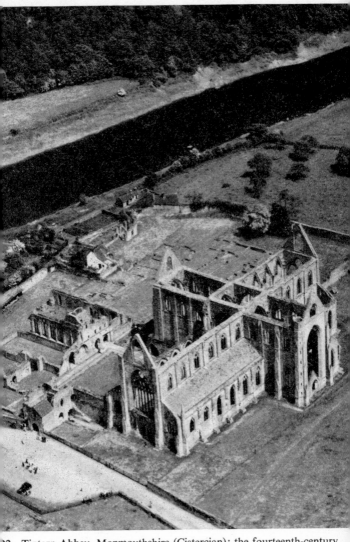

22 Tintern Abbey, Monmouthshire (Cistercian): the fourteenth-century
church and monastic buildings

23 Milton Abbey, Dorset (Benedictine): the fourteenth-century choir

24 Westminster Abbey (Benedictine): the
thirteenth-century choir and presbytery

25 Bristol Cathedral, originally St Augustine's Abbey (Augustinian): Abbot Newbury's tomb

26 St Bartholomew's Priory, Smithfield, London (Augustinian): in the Norman ambulatory

27 Christchurch Priory, Hampshire (Augustinian): the early sixteenth-century choir-stalls

28 Worcester Cathedral Priory (Benedictine), fourteenth century

REFECTORIES

29 Beaulieu Abbey, Hampshire (Cistercian): the thirteenth-century
reader's pulpit

30 An intact interior: Edington Priory, Wiltshire (Bonshommes)

31 The Carthusian plan: Mount Grace Priory, Yorkshire, showing the monks' separate cells and, in the foreground, the church and 'communal buildings

were sometimes, in documents, styled *cementarii* or *lathotomi*. There were also the layers, setters, and wallers, and the rough masons and hard hewers (or scapplers) who dressed the large stone blocks and were responsible for the rough types of masonry, apart from the portions carried out in worked or dressed stone. The carpenters, as distinct from the more wandering masons, were guild men, as their occupation was a settled one in a society where most domestic architecture was of timber framing and clay. They were required for making templates for the masons, for building lodges for the workmen, and for erecting scaffolding, falsework, and centering for vault construction, as well as the massive timberwork of the outer roof above a vault. The diggers and carters were also local men.

The erection of a monastery was no light undertaking. Apart from the church, there were, as we have seen, the numerous adjacent buildings, together with drainage, water-supply, fishponds, enclosing walls, and gates. In many smaller houses it was comparatively easy, when allowing for initial capital expenditure on the part of founders, to complete most of the buildings in one operation, but in most larger monasteries it was beyond the capacity of any one house, even if richly endowed, to provide funds for the whole work to be carried through without a break. Three examples of large-scale building are here given from surviving chronicles and fabric rolls. The first is an account of the rebuilding of the choir at Canterbury Cathedral after the disastrous fire (seen as divine retribution for Becket's murder) which burnt out the Norman choir in 1174. The second notes the rebuilding of the choir and presbytery at Westminster by Henry

III between 1245 and 1270. The third tells of the foundation of Vale Royal by Edward I, the building being carried out between 1277 and 1281, and the Cistercian community first planted at Darnhall being moved to the new site.

The graphic account in the tract by Gervase the monk "On the burning and repair of the Church at Canterbury" remains our earliest and best account of English mediaeval building activity. The disaster started on September 5th, 1174. After a graphic account of the beginning and spread of the fire, and of the gutting of the eastern limb of the Norman cathedral, Gervase continues as follows: "Bethink what might grief oppressed the heart of the sons of the church under this tribulation; truly that they might alleviate their miseries with a little consolation, they put together as well as they could, an altar and station in the nave, where they might wail rather than sing their services, and so the brethren remained in grief and sorrow for five years, separated from the people only by a low wall. Meanwhile the brethren sought counsel as to how the burnt church might be repaired, but without success; for the pillars were weakened by the heat and were scaling in places, so that they frightened even the wisest out of their wits. French and English artificers were summoned, but these differed in opinion. Some said they could repair the pillars, without mischief to the walls above, others that the whole church must be pulled down. However, amongst them was a certain William of Sens, a Man active and ready, and as a workman most skilful both in wood and stone. Him therefore they retained, on account of his lively genius and good reputation and dismissed the others. And he

114

residing many days with the monks carefully surveyed the walls, yet did for some time conceal the truth from them for fear it would kill them. But he went on preparing all things needful for the work and when the monks were somewhat comforted ventured to tell them the truth and at length they agreed to the total destruction of the choir. He then procured stone from beyond the sea, constructing ingenious machines for loading and unloading ships and drawing cement and stones. He made moulds for shaping the stones for the sculptors assembled, and diligently prepared other things of the same kind, and the choir was pulled down and nothing else done that year."

It is interesting to note from this account how the differences of opinion at Canterbury as to whether or not the ruined piers could be made good was repeated later after the destruction of old St Paul's in the Great Fire of London in 1666. What actually happened at Canterbury was that the outer walls of "Conrad's Glorious Choir" were largely preserved, and remain to this day as the Norman shell inside which a new choir was fashioned in Transitional Gothic. Gervase is not quite accurate when he speaks of the "total destruction" and pulling down of the late Norman choir. He goes on to describe in detail the progress of the work in the first two years of rebuilding. In the third year we find that "in the summer, commencing from the cross (i.e. the central crossing), he erected ten pillars, being five on each side. Upon these he placed the arches and vaults. And having completed both sides of the triforia and clerestories, was at the beginning of the fourth year in the act of preparing with machines for the turning of the great vault, when suddenly the beams broke under his feet, and he fell to the ground, stones and timbers accompanying his fall from the upper vault, say fifty feet. Thus sorely bruised by the blows from the beams and stones, he was rendered helpless alike to himself and for his work, but no other person than himself was in the least injured. Against the master only was this vengeance of God or spite of the devil directed. The master thus hurt remained in his bed under medical care in expectation of recovering, but was deceived. Nevertheless, as the winter approached, he gave charge of the work to a certain ingenious and industrious monk who was overseer of the masons; an appointment whence much envy and malice arose, because it made this young man appear more skilful than richer and more powerful ones. But the master reclining in bed commanded all things that should be done in order. In these operations the fourth year was occupied and the beginning of the fifth. And the master, perceiving that he derived no benefit from the physicians, gave up his work, and crossing the sea, returned to his home in France. And another succeeded him in the charge of the works, William by name, English by nation, small in body, but in workmanship acute and honest."

One notes from this narrative that in the twelfth century working architects were employed to design monastic churches and buildings. They were selected by competition, and chosen for their capacity for a special undertaking. Only one monk (perhaps Gervase himself) is mentioned as having anything to do with the construction, and he is spoken of as the overseer of the masons.

The second work to be noticed is the rebuilding of

the eastern half of Westminster Abbey by Henry III between 1245 and 1269. It forms, of course, a somewhat special case owing to the particular interest of the monarch himself, and from its consequent treatment very much as a "government job". The king was a wilful, headstrong monarch with a passion for building and for the collection of art treasures; St Edward the Confessor being his patron saint, he from the first lavished gifts on his shrine and church, and willed his body to be buried beside that of his patron. It is therefore not surprising that he conceived the idea of a church comparable with the great French buildings such at Rheims, Amiens and Beauvais. He made preliminary preparations by ordering the sheriff of Kent to provide a hundred barges for the conveyance of stone, and that all stone for London should be diverted to Westminster; also that all persons having grey stone for sale should take it to the abbey. The eastern part of the Confessor's church had first to be demolished, after which a start was made on July 6th, 1245. There was no question of any lack of funds so long as the king was kept in good humour. He appointed his master-mason, his master-carpenter, and his clerk of works, Edward of Westminster. The master-mason was Henry of Reynes, probably an Englishman but much influenced by French examples at Rheims and elsewhere. He died in 1253; John of Gloucester succeeded him, who in turn gave place to Robert of Beverley, all of them being the King's master-masons who looked after the royal palaces and castles, in addition to the work at Westminster Abbey. The eager and impatient monarch expended money at the rate of £2,000 a year, and from time to time issued orders

117

for the expedition of the work, as in 1250 when he commanded that at least six to eight hundred men should be at work on the building. The dedication of the new building took place on October 13, 1269, after twenty-five years of labour at a cost of £50,000. Here as at Canterbury there is no mention of monks, with the single exception of the King's beloved painter, Master William of Winchester.

Our third example is of the erection of a large convent remote from either town or village. As it was a new foundation, started from the beginning on a virgin site, there were none of the difficulties and complications normal when an existing church was being repaired or rebuilt. Again we have a royal foundation, and the fabric rolls for the first three years have been preserved. Edward I, owing to a threatened shipwreck, vowed to found a monastery to the glory of God, and he turned for help to the Cistercian Abbey Dore in Herefordshire, whose monks had shown him former kindness. A nucleus left Dore for Darnhall in Cheshire, which after a time proving unsuitable, they chose another site near the River Weaver in the Vale Royal of England. In 1277 the foundation-stones were laid with great pomp by the King and his Consort. He had set apart moneys for the work from his Palatinate of Cheshire, and appointed Leonius his collector to manage the financial side. The fabric rolls for the three years he was in charge are full of interesting details. The master-mason was Walter of Hereford, who had also charge of several other royal buildings. He received in wages two shillings a day; his assistant John of Battle three shillings a week, other masons being paid from half-a-crown downwards. The total number of masons employed during this time was 131, and they came from all quarters of England; their average stay being but for a few months, when they moved on to another lodge. Their names suggest the places of their origin; only seven came from cities and towns, the others from country districts or the neighbourhood of abbeys where building construction was being carried out on a large scale.

During these early years the time was spent upon foundations and walls, fine masonry for windows and arches being in a tentative state. Nevertheless, the quantity of stone quarried and brought to the site was extraordinary. The quarries were six miles distant, and during the period under review 35,448 loads of stone were carried. In addition to the masons, carpenters and carters, large gangs of diggers, quarrymen and smiths were employed. The cost to the king amounted to £1,000 a year, and his total outlay is said to have been over £32,000. The monks left Darnhall in 1281 for a small temporary building, evidently constructed of timber near the new site, as the carpenters were busily engaged erecting lodges for the workmen and the monks. They cut out of the Forest of Delamere 12,800 boards, for which 67,000 nails were provided. Laths and clay were also used.

The monks did not enter into their new home until 1330, and building operations continued beyond that date. The Black Prince, who as Earl of Chester had a special interest in any abbey in the County Palatine, gave substantial help in 1353 and 1358. Then in 1359 onwards the Black Prince set in train the complete rebuilding of the eastern limb, on a magnificent apsidal plan with a chevet of radiating chapels.

In none of the above three undertakings was there any lack of funds, but this was by no means always the case. If a monastery was unable to rely on such windfalls as offerings at the shrines of saints or political heroes, as at Canterbury, Gloucester, or Hayles, or on private or royal benefactors, but had to fall back on its own limited resources of regular income, major building operations could become a hopeless struggle, and at times even necessary repairs remained undone. An important monastery such as Westminster found it impossible to carry out projected schemes without energetic outside backing, as the endeavour to complete Westminster's nave sufficiently shows; in this case, of course, the effect of wars and political disturbances on the royal finances was a potent factor. After Henry III had completed the new eastern half, the Confessor's nave remained for over a hundred years, abutting against the new work. Then in 1376 the will of Cardinal Simon Langham, who had been abbot of Westminster before being Archbishop of Canterbury and later a Cardinal in Curia, provided funds for Abbot Litlington to proceed with a new nave, the early Norman nave being demolished while the outer walls of the new one were being built. The King continued to take great practical and financial interest in the operations, and in 1393 we find that Richard II empowered "the King's workers of marble columns in Westminster Abbey" to impress masons, workmen, and transport facilities in the Isle of Purbeck. But the work was seriously delayed by such factors as the French wars and the Wars of the Roses. The nave and its western towers remained incomplete when the abbey was dissolved, and the famous western towers were finished in their present form by Hawksmoor in the eighteenth century. The master-masons during the late mediaeval period included Henry Yevele, William of Colchester, John of Thirsk, and Robert Stowell.

There are many points of interest in the actual building of monasteries. At Vale Royal the stone for the abbey was conveyed in carts, there being no suitable waterways or rivers, but in the wilds of Yorkshire, during the middle of the twelfth century, the abbey of Rievaulx, under Abbot Ailred, constructed waterways to convey their stone to the building. They made rough sledge roads down the hill-sides to the valley to dams or small harbours, and from thence cut canals to the site, using the water from the small River Rye to float their stone. Water transport was of the utmost importance to the builders of great mediaeval churches (indeed it so remained till the railway age), and the Fenland waterways were of particular value, as they made it possible for the good building stone of the limestone belt to be taken to the stoneless districts of the eastern counties. Sea transport was also of importance in this same connexion, and southern monasteries like those at Winchester and Christchurch found it easier to ship stone from Caen in Normandy than to get it from elsewhere in England.

Apart from the churches, many monastic buildings were at first constructed of timber; excavations at Winchester in the summer of 1961 showed that this was the case with the early Norman buildings of the cathedral priory. It was a long process converting them into stone construction and this, along with the early prevalance of timber roofs over the actual churches, accounts for the numerous fires which are recorded. At Croxden, in 1332 to 1334, the general reroofing of the buildings was done with over 70,000 wooden shingles. At Bury, in 1150, practically all the conventual buildings were consumed by fire, and during a riot in 1327 they were again burnt. At Milton, in 1309, the whole of the Norman church was gutted and had to be partially replaced by the present building.

Just as in systematic planning and construction the monasteries were apt to be ahead of their time, so too they were pioneers with regard to water supply and drainage. At Christ Church, Canterbury, as early as the twelfth century there was a complete water-supply conveyed through lead pipes, of which the plan has been preserved in the library of Trinity College, Cambridge. The source was outside the north wall of the city, and the water was first taken to a tower, then passing under the city walls it fed the lavatories, cisterns, bath-house, kitchen and fish-ponds of the convent. Before coming into the city it passed through five filter beds, so constructed as to be easily cleaned out. At various places it could be drawn off by means of stop-cocks; in the people's cemetery, there was a pedestal fixed to enable it to be taken by dipping in a pail; and the conduit-house a column to give a head pressure to the water. At Chester in 1285 the water for the convent was conveyed three miles from Christleton, where a tank twenty feet square was constructed, with another in the cloister, a pipe being laid between the two; the king granted permission for the pipe to be laid through any intervening land. At Waverley in 1215, when the spring from which the monks obtained their supply suddenly dried up, "not without great astonishment", Symon the monk searched and at last found a spring six hundred yards from the east end of the buildings. "After great difficulty, enquiry and invention, and not without much labour and sweating he brought it by underground channels to the offices of the abbey". It was usual first to make an accumulating cistern at the source and then convey the water through lead pipes (which were welded, not drawn) to a conduit and there re-distribute it to the various offices. At Beaulieu, hollowed elm trunks were used for the main supply to the conduit-house; the latter still exists, circular in plan, twelve feet in diameter, with a plain domed roof. The friaries also gave much thought to the same problem. One of the friary conduits at Bristol is still in working order, though the friary buildings have disappeared, and at Cambridge the famous fountain in the Great Court at Trinity College is supplied by the conduit which originally brought water to the Franciscan site now occupied by Sidney Sussex. Other excellent monastic supplies were at Mount Grace, the London Charterhouse, Rievaulx, and the cathedral priories at Durham, Winchester, and Worcester.

A stream for flushing away sewerage and other refuse was an essential element in a monastic site. We have seen how the siting of the domestic buildings would often be determined by these considerations. If the stream or artificial channel flowed in direct proximity to the buildings it was split up so as to run under the infirmary, latrine block, and kitchens. Otherwise, where the monastic buildings stood on slightly rising ground as at Evesham, Keynsham, and Ely, special sewers had to be built to connect with the rivers; the underground passages which one is told were secret means of access to nunneries or castles are really the remains of these great drains. Split streams and drainage systems can be well studied in the ruined abbeys of Furness, Whalley, Reading, and elsewhere.

7

Monasteries and Society

IN the first flush of their enthusiasm the monasteries more than justified their existence. They were the fortresses amidst a world of savagery, where learning was preserved, worship continued and the arts encouraged. They taught the Western world the uses of agriculture in supplying the needs of men instead of having to rely upon the chase. By their example they gradually educated the people in law and order, and in the advantages of a continuous system in place of the haphazard methods then prevalent.

For many centuries the monasteries were in advance of their time in such matters as the planning, furnishing, and conduct of their houses. They were virtually the only places where the inhabitants lived according to a rule, each individual having specific duties, and in which a community dwelt together in amity, without small differences ending in strife and bloodshed. The monastery was a house of well-ordered quietness, and it is not surprising that men fled to these oases in a desert of tumult; for a military profession was the only one open to a noble or a freeman, and learning apart from religion was almost unknown.

The monasteries also espoused the honour of labour, then considered only fit for slaves or serfs. They taught it by example, tilling the fields and gardens, doing humble work of all kinds, worshipping God whilst labouring in the fields as well as in the church. These early ideals were not, however, of long observance, for as the monasteries became wealthy and powerful, and as they inevitably became integrated into the general fabric of society, their rigidity tended, except for the Carthusians and others already mentioned to fall into abeyance. Their early popularity made for their undoing. Lands and money were lavished on them, their establishments became too numerous for a generally high standard of vocational fervour, and they became tainted with the world and its ways. Again and again new orders arose, each harking back (as did the early Cluniacs, Cistercians, and Premonstratensians) to first principles. But as each grew in wealth their original ideas in most cases faded. To the last, however, they retained many good points. They still stood for community of life, and the world had learnt much of what they had set out to teach. The fault of the older monastic orders, by the time of the coming of the friars, was that they looked inward instead of outward, being more interested in their own spiritual perfection than in leavening the masses. There was, of course, a proper place for those with a genuine coenobitic and contemplative vocation, but the numbers of professed religious came far to exceed the number of those likely in their own lives to embody the true monastic spirit.

LITERATURE AND THE ARTS

The early monastic libraries contained practically all the wealth of mediaeval literature, both in variety of content and in beauty of script and illumination. Many monks devoted a lifetime to writing a single volume such as the

Winchester Bible, which remained unfinished at the writer's death. The abbey of St Alban was famous not only for the production of books, but for services to writers, of whom Roger de Wendover and Matthew Paris may be singled out. Their chronicles, along with those of Florence of Worcester, William of Malmesbury, and others are still among the foundations on which mediaevalists build their studies. The size of monastic libraries can be gauged by the catalogue of the Canterbury manuscripts, made between 1285 and 1331, which enumerates 1850. Durham possessed 921 volumes, and several catalogues from other convents show how large was their scope. All these libraries remained until the suppression, when they were either wilfully destroyed or dispersed. The surviving treasures would have been even fewer had not some of the religious bought volumes for their own use which have since found their way into national and college libraries. In addition, the deliberate collecting activities of men like Archbishop Matthew Parker were fortunately started soon after the dissolution.

The monasteries, like the secular cathedrals and the other collegiate churches, were filled with the work of contemporary craftsmen who, but for their patronage, would never have had the chance to develop their art. The work commissioned included that of the glass-workers, craftsmen and carvers in wood, stone and ivory, smiths, painters and artists, gold and silver workers, tapestry weavers and embroiderers. Hence the establishment of guilds of craftsmen partly owing their origin and livelihood to the orders given by the monastic houses.

We have seen how the monasteries were, to a large extent, the hotels and inns of the Middle Ages. The standards of cleanliness and order in monastic guesthouses were apt to be considerably higher than in many households and inns outside, with some consequent influence on the minds of those who stayed in them. We have also seen how monastic hospitality was often seriously abused. Members of the upper classes were often entertained at the abbots' tables (where the rules against meat eating were greatly relaxed), and the feasts recorded in the chronicles accounted for incredible quantities of food. The installation feast of a new abbess of Wilton in 1299 called for the serving of swans, peacocks, and venison, to say nothing of two thousand eggs.

The record of monastic almsgiving is not really impressive in relation to the resources available. The monks did indeed support certain numbers of old bedesmen and women in almshouses and in the almonries, and at obits and anniversaries distributed bread, and occasionally money, while well-worn clothes were given to the poor. They were supposed to visit the sick in the neighbourhood of the monasteries and give them assistance, but this seems to have been more the exception than the rule; more often they took colour from the surrounding world in their outlook towards the down-trodden, and their sympathy towards the stricken was finer in theory than in practice. The mediaeval world was a sorry place for people without influence and without means; the monks like laymen followed the precept that a man should be content with the place God had provided for him, and not allow his mind to dwell on better things.

Neither did the monasteries, after their comparatively early period, take a strong lead in educational or intellectual matters. This was despite the fact that they sent some of their members to study at the Universities, and despite such items as the financing, by the nunnery of Wilton just before the dissolution, of exhibitioners at Oxford and Cambridge. They certainly taught their novices, and had schools for singing boys. But the outside world did not greatly share in these benefits. Sometimes poor boys, like little Nigel already mentioned in an item from the Westminster *compotus* rolls, were taught in the almonry. There are also records of free schools attached to some monasteries, and in certain towns grammar schools were founded by the abbots. These, along with the schools in which chantry priests taught, increased in number towards the close of the Middle Ages. After the suppression many were refounded under the name of the king or of those who had taken over the monastic estates.

LANDLORDS AND AGRICULTURISTS

From the first the monasteries were landowners, for their founders, in default of the financial methods by which endowments can be provided in modern society, endowed them with lands which were increased from time to time by gifts in respect of prayer to be offered for the donors' souls. These lands were some of them brought into new cultivation by the monks (especially the Cistercians) and were divided into waste, arable, and pasture. The tenants of each manor, as with those held by lay lords, had shares in each class. The waste land was in many manors by far the largest section, and was common to all for turf-cutting, wood-gathering, rough pasturage, and the mowing of hay. In time the abbeys brought more land into cultivation by clearing, ploughing and marling, making for the purpose clay-pits, which afterwards became the ponds still to be seen in the fields. This progress was discouraged by the realm and the lords by heavy fines imposed on any person who cultivated a new piece of land, especially if it interfered with hunting or encroached upon forests; the tenants also objected to forfeiting their rights in the common lands.

In the early feudal period, and on manors farmed "in demesne" by their monastic owners and not leased out, there were two types of tenant – money tenants and service tenants. The former, called the *censarii*, paid a money rent and were freed from the work required from the second class, but they had to find oxen for ploughing and extra labour for harvest. The service tenants were called villeins and usually held two bovates of land, eight bovates being enough for one plough. Their service was to work two days a week, find carts for carting, to plough twice a year and reap thrice in August, to fetch salt and fish and to pay for the use of the abbot's pasture land; and there were many restrictions and fines. Villeins could be sold with an estate, but could not be sold as chattels; they had also to pay a fine for obtaining the abbot's consent to a daughter's marriage. Comparing the position of the villeins on the manors of the lords, the convents, and the king, Coulton thinks that the monastic villeins were better off than under the lords but not so well off as under the king. The religious were more humane in their treatment, but this was counterbalanced by their innate conservativeness; the manner of treatment depended also upon the individual character of the abbot. At the Premonstratensian abbey of Titchfield those who worked all day at harvest time received, about 3 p.m., bread with beer or cider, broth and meat or fish as well as a drink after dinner, and for supper a wheaten loaf and some sort of fish. On the other hand no food was apt to be given on secular manors except on special occasions.

Other tenants were the *bovarii* and the *cotsetti*. The former looked after the abbot's ploughs and oxen, and generally held two bovates of land; the latter were the cottagers and labourers who worked one day a week for the abbot. Finally came the actual slaves or *servi* who were liable for service and held no connexion with the land; they were bought and sold as mere chattels; but it is considered by some authorities that this class was extinct towards the close of the thirteenth century. All these grades of tenants were in a state of bondage or serfdom, though in some degree removed from actual slavery. It is curious that in the eyes of the law they all had very few liberties, but in actual practice they enjoyed by custom substantial rights. But the following instances show the insecurity of the rural workers' legal position and the tendency of the monasteries to push to the uttermost what they considered their legal rights even in regard to the lives of their workers and their children. At Whalley in 1289 a serf was sold for a hundred shillings with all his brood. William Dives gave the monks of Eynsham, "Richard Rowland, who was my born serf with all his brood". In time, however, serfdom in England declined, and serfs, though still found, became far fewer, gradually buying their freedom.

We have seen how the abbots would have lay stewards or bailiffs to manage their manors and preside at the manor courts. The abbot, as a lord entitled to administer justice to his own tenants, kept his own gallows and stocks and maintained order through his own officials. As with the estates in lay hands the whole organization of dependent manors centred round the monastic owners and was primarily framed to meet their requirements. If the tenants' various services on the abbey lands were not performed the land reverted to the abbot. One must, however, remember that by the end of the monastic period many manors were farmed out on long leases to prosperous and rising yeomen or small gentry, with little detailed interference by the landlords provided the rents came in. The small scale tenants lived in villages and appointed the ablest man in each village to look after their interests. He was called the foreman or reeve (a title also sometimes used for the monastic supervisor), and was often in opposition to the abbot's bailiff.

The abbot's woods also brought in revenue, especially in the autumn when the beech nuts and acorns fell. All villages kept pigs, which generally had to find their own living; but in the autumn, by payment either in money or in kind, the villagers were allowed the privilege of turning their swine into the woods. In 1279 the pannage of the woods was handed to the Abbot of Vale Royal, who received sixty-two and sixpence and eighty pigs valued at eight pounds. In 1325 the abbot sold the season's acorns of Bradford Wood to Richard of Buckelegh, who turned forty swine into the woods. A neighbouring squire broke down the fences, seized Richard's swine and put fifty of his own in their place. The abbot's servants seized these pigs and the squire then entered into litigation with the abbot, but failed. The abbot's woods were useful for hunting, providing a pastime for himself and his friends. In 1258 there was a dispute between Hugh, prior of Kirkham, and William de Rhos, as to the right of the prior, who was hunting in the said wood with his dogs, "to wit limers, brachets and hare hounds, and taking all manner of beasts, to wit stags, harts, hinds, foxes and hares. The prior says his predecessors have hunted time beyond memory until five years ago."

When reading of the people's attempts to free themselves from the yoke of the feudal system, we must remember that the monasteries, as landlords, were only a part of that system. However, though they might be more lenient, and were less capricious masters than some of the lay aristocracy, the ecclesiastical corporations, monastic or otherwise, were irremovable (till Henry VIII's ecclesiastical revolution) by political means and remained conservative to the last in maintaining their legal rights. In this they were helped by their superior literary education, and by their more efficient system of keeping and codifying their charters, deeds, and other documents of title It was no accident that documents (like those of the University of Cambridge in the townsmen's rising of 1381) were a prime target of those who rose in forcible rebellion against ecclesiastical rule.

From the thirteenth century onwards one hears of violent and brutal acts against monastic landlords and their representatives. At Dunstable, in 1229, there was a rebellion over tallage, the rebels declaring, when excommunicated, that they would go to hell sooner than be beaten.

In 1280 the villein tenants of Burton on Trent brought an unsuccessful action against the abbot, claiming rights as free tenants. In 1309 the Abbot of Combermere was assaulted at Nantwich, one of his monks slain, his grange burnt, and his goods stolen. During the enquiry the people took on such a threatening attitude that the abbot dared not return to his abbey. In 1330 at Vale Royal one of the abbot's servants was murdered, and the men who assaulted him cut off his head and played football with it. The Peasants' Revolt of 1381 saw several serious disturbances, particularly in some of the monastic boroughs. At Bury St Edmund's (where there had been many previous outbreaks) the serfs and bondsmen seized the prior, condemned him, and cut off his head. At St Albans there were severe tumults and the abbey was besieged.

A striking instance in this struggle for freedom was made by the villeins of Darnhall, a manor of Vale Royal. As early as the founder's days they appealed to the king against the oppression of the abbot but without success; they made further complaint in 1307 with the same result. In 1329 they broke into open insurrection, and were tried by the abbot's court, not as plaintiffs, but as prisoners judged by the defendant. They were put in shackles and their property confiscated. In 1336 a renewal of their appeal to the king and parliament met with the same fate; however, meeting the abbot, who barely escaped with his life, on his return through Rutland, they killed his groom. They were then hauled before the king at Stamford, and compelled to make abject submission.

The Statute of Mortmain, introduced by Edward I, was an attempt to control further gifts to religious foundations. If such gifts were made, a licence was required. Lands and other endowments continued to be given, but at a price. There was an added penalty in that all estates given without a licence were forfeit to the Crown.

Gifts were not often made to monastic houses unconditionally, as they were generally given to secure the saying of masses and other prayers for the souls of the donors and their ancestors. If they were given without a licence the ensuing forfeiture annulled the gift, thus imperilling the souls of the benefactors. The Statute of Mortmain made it more difficult to present land or money. Upon application for a licence the sheriff had to call together a jury to examine all the facts, assess the value of the gift, and estimate how far the Crown was being deprived of taxes and emoluments, and in the event of a licence being granted, the size of the fine had to be fixed. These fines do not appear to have borne any relation to the value of the land, and we do not know by what methods they were levied. They could be quite high, as one sees when in 1393 the priory of Castle Acre appropriated two East Anglian livings, the fee on this occasion being the very considerable sum of eighty marks. In many instances, however, people who had benefited the State were let off lightly, especially if the king was interested in the monastery concerned. Monasteries also acquired land by purchase, exchanging them when this was mutually beneficial, and made pensions and small grants to bishops and others in compensation for the appropriation of churches. In all these cases a licence had to be obtained and a fee paid.

The Crown thus gained power over some of the financial activities of religious houses, and fees for licences in Mortmain were a frequent and useful source of government income. In view of the pious nature of donations, prohibition of benefactions would have raised a storm from the clergy and laity alike; but the Crown obtained power to ensure that the donor's stipulations were carried out. If it was proved that these conditions had been neglected, the gift could be made void. If the gift was entered upon before the licence was granted and the fine paid, a pardon had to be sought, and when granted, involved further expense.

MONASTERIES IN THE TOWNS
The association of a monastery with a town in which it was placed grew difficult as the town developed, and led either to riotous behaviour or a sullen resistance to the rights of the abbot. At first the villages were glad of their protection, the domination of an abbey being a help; but as trade developed the burgesses became restive and attempted to free themselves from the abbot's restrictions, with his rights of toll and fairs, fees and elections.

Reading remained under the rule of the abbot for 250 years. During the whole time the abbot maintained all his rights, the town struggling unsuccessfully to throw them off, resulting in constant friction and disputes. The inhabitants were bound hand and foot, for he was the owner of the streams, fisheries, mills and soil. He held the markets, controlled trade and supervised the manufacture of cloth; he appointed the mayor and lesser officials, exercising his veto for admission to the guild. The entire administration of justice was in his hands, fines being imposed for any and every breach of his laws, and he reserved to himself the symbols of office. Constant appeals to the king were unavailing, for the king and the abbot worked together for a common end. All abbeys were not, however, like those at Bury and Reading. At Burton on Trent they seem always to have been fairly popular. They paved the streets, provided a market hall and a conduit, and founded a grammar school a few years before the suppression. As towns developed near some of the more important abbeys resentment was felt against the right of the abbots to hold fairs. In Staffordshire, for instance, there were complaints from the burgesses of Stafford, Lichfield, and Tutbury concerning those at Burton and Abbot's Bromley. The abbey of Chester to some extent escaped the bitter hostility shown elsewhere. Defeated in their early attempts to enlarge their trading rights, they made concessions and tried to conciliate the burgesses. They also started mystery plays for the gratification of the town and in other ways maintained goodwill.

The abbeys would help towns in other ways. Where their precincts abutted on town walls it was their duty to keep their sections in repair and provide defenders, as at Chester, Winchester, and Gloucester. The Priory of Dover, in 1476 was called upon to keep the town's cannon "ready with powder and stones and other stuff as they used to do". The maintainance of bridges and roads was a religious duty, the abbots doing their share, especially when they connected up their estates. At Ely, which was surrounded by fen and swamp, they built several bridges and constructed roads to enable pilgrims to reach the monastery, every bridge having its toll-keeper, the revenues going to the sacrist. In the fourteenth century the Abbot of Chester made an agreement with the neighbouring lords as to the repair of several bridges in the district. In 1283 Crowland and Spalding constructed many bridges. In the thirteenth century the Abbot of Whitby built a permanent bridge over the Esk. On the other hand the Abbot of Fountains in 1313 refused to repair the bridge at Bradeley, and in 1368 the Prior of Nostell was ordered to repair two bridges at Birstall and Batley, being the rector of both places, but complained that none of his predecessors had been bound to do so.

EXTERNAL RELATIONSHIPS

Relations between the monastic houses themselves were not always smooth, and many cases of litigation occurred. The Cistercian abbey of Sawley, in the extreme West of Yorkshire, appealed against the foundation, not far across the Lancashire border at Whalley, of another abbey of its own Order. But there does not seem to have been any trouble between Rievaulx and Byland which were even closer neighbours. Matters would sometimes become more serious when there was a struggle between a dependant priory and its mother house. For instance, Monk Bretton in Yorkshire was founded under the Cluniac priory of Pontefract, the Abbot of Cluny giving Monk Bretton the right to elect its own prior, should the prior of Pontefract be present. To this Pontefract would not agree and the most unseemly quarrels with armed interference took place, especially when Pontefract took possession of Bretton and imprisoned the monks. Papal bulls and verdicts of commissions had no effect on this state of affairs, which after temporary lulls broke out with added bitterness, Pontefract electing priors from their own houses, Bretton repudiating them. Finally, about 1279, Bretton seceded from the Cluniacs and joined the Benedictines.

Monastic relations with the nobility and gentry can be judged from such matters as benefactions, litigation, and the participation of the gentry and yeomanry in monastic administration. The records of litigation tend to make the most interesting reading, but one has to realize, as with modern crime reports which concern a publicised minority of the population, that court cases arose out of events which were abnormal, and not the usual routine. The general picture, especially by the end of the monastic period, is of the monasteries' more or less complete integration into the general fabric of a society mainly made up of country landowners.

Owing to the loose way in which land boundaries were defined (with the complete absence of what we should call accurate maps and plans) there was constant friction, with many charges of trespass and encroachment. Rights of way were called into question, and disputed responsibility for the repair of roads and bridges led to quarrels. Manorial lords (and abbots) would sometimes take the law into their own hands, and conflicts would start between their armed retainers.

The following examples of trouble are mainly taken from the records of Cheshire or Staffordshire monasteries, but the episodes can be paralleled elsewhere. In 1277 the Abbot of Egglestone (a Premonstratensian house in Yorkshire) sued Henry de Stanley and others for throwing down the abbot's mill at Chardehale, and doing other enormities to the damage of a hundred shillings. In 1320 a plea was lodged for John Lewis, cellarer of Vale Royal, who on his return after transacting business at Chester, was set upon at Tarvin by seven men from Northwich, and barely escaped with his life. In 1334 the Prior of Tutbury was captured on his way home from visiting the bishop, and the men were solemnly cursed from the altar. At Croxden in 1319 the new lord of Alverton demanded from the monks a daily distribution of alms, the keeping of his horses and hounds to any number he pleased, the maintaining every Friday of seven of his bailiffs with a room for their use. On refusal he captured 160 of the convent's sheep, twenty oxen and thirty-two horses, so that the monks were unable to plough or sow.

The other side of this picture of turbulence and discord is the way in which the monasteries were closely linked, by ties both of blood and social obligation, to the upper and middle classes of mediaeval society. We have seen how local gentry would often help in the administration of monastic estates. It was very easy, for those from whose families the abbots' bailiffs and seneschals had long been drawn, and for the men who, as tenants, had long been the occupants on the spot of the monastic manors, to step into the monks' granges, or even abbots' lodges, when the suppression came. Kinship would often reinforce bonds of tenancy or paid service. So we find that at Cullompton in East Devon the manorial lordship was vested in the Cistercian abbey of Buckland near Plymouth. A few years before the dissolution the local

140

clothier who was the abbey's bailiff was also a brother of the last abbot. From the same period we have the list of the twenty-six little girls who were taught, as they might be nowadays at a convent boarding school, in the well conducted, much respected Benedictine nunnery of St Mary's at Winchester. Bridget Plantagenet was a daughter of Lord Lisle and hence, through one of his indiscretions, a grand-daughter of King Edward IV. Her father was away abroad as Governor of Calais; he did not hesitate, in a few more years, to acquire the site of its dissolved Carmelite friary. Of the other girls some were the children of knights, and the local squires provided the other pupils, two of them Tichbornes of the famous family still living a few miles away. There were, indeed, many patrons and clients of the monks who would soon gleefully enlarge their properties from the great parcelling out of what had long sustained the ordered life of choir and cloister. But for the moment, and for centuries past, the religious and the lay landlords had co-existed with reasonable ease as parts of the same social establishment.

8

The Suppression and After

By the time of the general suppression under Henry VIII the religious houses in England and Wales had been somewhat reduced below the peak figure attained by about 1350. But the various suppressions carried out between the fourteenth century and the 1530s in no way corresponded to the wholesale dissolution achieved by Henry VIII; the lands and revenues of the religious houses which disappeared in pre-Reformation times were nearly all transferred to other ecclesiastical establishments and not used for the enrichment of a new generation of lay gentry and noblemen.

The first important example of these pre-Reformation suppressions was in 1312 when the Templars were dissolved, not only in England but universally, by Papal decree. Most of the Templars' property was, however, in due course transferred to the Knights Hospitallers.

More complex, and with a strongly political undertone, was the eventual fate of the "alien priories", and the other estates in England, Wales, and the Channel Islands which belonged to religious houses in Normandy and elsewhere in France. With the political separation, in the reign of John, of England and Normandy the mother houses of these alien priories not already in French territory became politically a part of France.

The relationship between the parent abbeys and the daughter houses became ever more difficult with the growing frequency of Anglo-French wars. The Cluniacs and the Grammontines, with their marked dependency on Cluny and Grammont (particularly over the appointment of new priors) were also in an awkward position. The Premonstratensians and Cistercians also had difficulties arising from their close links with foreign headquarters, but both these groups escaped what befell the alien priories.

What happened, particularly during the periods of open war in the fourteenth century, was that the outright possessions of the French abbeys were often sequestered by the Crown; the estates so controlled in effect had what we should now call the status of "enemy property", but would return to their parent houses when periods of peace supervened. They were, moreover, in an increasingly false position. The final blow came under Henry V, when in 1414 an Act of Parliament gave authority for their permanent confiscation. The Cluniac houses, in the meantine, had become "denizen", or independent priories on the same basis as the English Benedictine houses, and no change, for the moment, was made in the organization of the White Canons. A few of the alien priories in fact survived as small conventual establishments till the reign of Henry VI. Others, like Boxgrove, Abergavenny, Chepstow, Tutbury, Holy Trinity Micklegate at York, and Tywardreath in Cornwall became "denizen" and continued, as ordinary Benedictine monasteries, till the general suppression. But the great majority ceased to exist as separate establishments. There was, however, no question of their permanent retention by the Crown, or of their grant as perquisites to royal favourites or lay landlords. Sooner or later these estates were transferred to other establishments of no less ecclesiastical character; any other course of action would have been inconceivable under monarchs as devout as were those of the House of Lancaster. Henry V's own foundations of Sheen and Syon were very largely endowed with lands which had formed part of French abbeys' estates, and most of the remaining properties were eventually made over to existing English monasteries such as Bruton, Tavistock, Mount Grace, and some of the other Carthusian priories, to secular Colleges like those at Fotheringhay, St George's Windsor, or St Stephen's at Westminster, and to such seats of learning as New College and All Souls at Oxford and Pembroke Hall at Cambridge. More important still was the way in which the dissolution of the alien priories helped the great new Colleges set up by Henry VI; the "royal and religious" foundations of Eton and of King's College at Cambridge could hardly, indeed, have been financed in any other way.

The fifteenth century also saw the extinction, through sheer inanition and inadequacy, of some small religious houses, particularly among the dimunitive priories of the Augustinian canons. Examples of this "fading out" were the priories of Longleat in Wiltshire and Chetwode in Buckinghamshire; in the former case the lands were handed to the Carthusians of Hinton. The same process continued, uncontroversially from the religious point of view, in the sixteenth century, for as late as 1533 the small Somerset priory of Stavordale became a "cell" of the larger Augustinian house at Taunton.

Lacock Abbey, Wiltshire (Augustinian Canonesses): the south walk
of the fifteenth-century cloisters

33 Bayham Abbey, Sussex (Premonstratensian): a general view

34 Abbotsbury Abbey, Dorset (Benedictine): the fifteenth-century abbey barn

Hexham Priory, Northumberland (Augustinian): the night stairs

36 Glastonbury, Somerset: the early sixteenth century Abbot's Tribunal

37 Much Wenlock Priory, Shropshire (Cluniac): the infirmary and the prior's house

38 Brecon (Dominicans): the thirteenth-century choir

THE FRIARS

39 Bristol (Dominicans): remains of the cloisters

40 A monastic college: the *camerae* of Gloucester Hall (Benedictine), now Worcester College, Oxford

41 Newstead Priory, Nottinghamshire (Augustinian): Gothic Ruin and Stately Home

2 An Anglican Community (Society of the Sacred Mission): the chapel,
by C. C. Thompson, at Kelham, Nottinghamshire

43 The Benedictines revived: Downside Abbey, Somerset. Choir by Thomas Garner; nave by Sir Giles Gilbert Scott

Some small and inefficient religious houses were also suppressed by reforming bishops in the interest of new places of learning; no violence was thus done to the Church as a whole. Just before the end of the fifteenth century Bishop Alcock of Ely procured the suppression of St Radegund's nunnery at Cambridge, the buildings and lands becoming those of Jesus College. The saintly Bishop Fisher of Rochester suppressed two wretched little Benedictine nunneries for the augmentation of St John's College at Cambridge; the same process was carried much further, with his overriding authority as Papal Legate, by Cardinal Wolsey.

The suppressions carried out and planned by Wolsey formed part, and financially speaking an essential part, of his plans to found Colleges at Oxford and Ipswich. Between 1524 and 1529 no less than twenty-nine houses of monks, nuns, and canons regular were suppressed; further schemes were in hand at the time of the Cardinal's fall. Most of the establishments thus abolished were very small, but some were of moderate size, including Bayham, Daventry, and the Augustinian priory of St Frideswide at Oxford. The site of St Frideswide's was to be that of Cardinal College, and most of its beautiful church remains as the College chapel, and Cathedral, of Christ Church.

Thomas Wolsey was a brilliant administrator, with ideas for necessary reforms in the Church, as well as being a statesman of great ability. He well knew how ramshackle and unsatisfactory was the disposition of the English dioceses. Some of them, particularly that of Lincoln which Wolsey himself had held, were far too large, while others were small, weak, and poorly endowed.

Late in his career the Cardinal had plans for the subdivision of some large dioceses, and for the creation of new bishoprics to be financed, and their cathedrals provided, from the revenues of a few large abbeys. But Wolsey's fall and death came too soon for him to proceed to these larger, more significant suppressions; we shall see how some elements of his policy were achieved not by the Cardinal-Legate but by the King as Head of the English Church.

By 1530, with Henry VIII now set on the divorce of Queen Catherine, the religious houses of England stood on the eve of a doom which few could reasonably foresee. Their inmates were fairly numerous, worship in their churches continued with dignity if without recollective fervour, their buildings were often being reconstructed or adorned. Many, of course, had fallen far below their first ideals. They were far too numerous, and some were so rotten in their conduct as to merit little but abolition. But the picture of their infamy, at the time and in the pages of later writers, was coloured too dark, and by some deliberately so. Visiting bishops had indeed found much to blame in these last decades of English monasticism, and the houses of really fervent observance were painfully few. But Professor Knowles has well pointed out the wide differences between the findings of bishops whose care it was to amend and not to abolish, and the reports, compiled in 1535 and early in 1536, of the Royal Commissioners who sometimes took care to discover what their master wanted them to find. There could be no doubt, as men like Fisher and Wolsey had seen, that the monasteries and nunneries of England stood in grave need of pruning and reform. But pruning and reform re not the same as uprooting and revolution. It was revolution, not reform, that was the monasteries' fate. The cathedral priories, a dozen perhaps of the larger Benedictine abbeys, some houses of the Cistercians and of the canons regular, and a fair number of the nunneries could certainly have been spared to fit in with the religious régime established by Henry VIII. Any genuine reform of the English Church would certainly have spared the devout and spiritually minded establishments of the Carthusians, Bridgettines, Observant Friars, and Poor Clares. But these houses of high principle, as it happened, were among those the soonest and most savagely suppressed.

Their easy acceptance, in 1534, of the Royal Supremacy in Church affairs had, indeed, placed most of the monasteries in a somewhat false position. The Observant Friars had stood firm on this issue, and their friaries did not long survive their inmates' obduracy. But the Carthusians, after Prior Houghton in London and some others had been removed by execution, were induced to comply; so too were most of the Bridgettines of Syon. In 1535, with its sharp revelation of the financial and economic benefits, as distinct from spiritual or political results, which could flow to the government from a general suppression, the *Valor Ecclesiasticus* gave the king and Thomas Cromwell his minister a full and detailed record of the endowed value of Church lands and spiritual revenues. It was this *Valor*, in 1536 after the due digestion of the Commissioners' reports, which gave Henry and Cromwell their financial rule of thumb for the first great wave of new-style suppressions.

The basis of the suppressions carried out in 1536 was

that all houses whose net annual income was less than £200 were due for dissolution. Good and bad alike were supposedly covered, and there was no question now of the property of those that fell being diverted to other Church purposes. The Crown, and then various laymen, were the recipients of most of what now became available.

To a certain extent this first batch of dissolutions could have been interpreted as a measure of monastic reform. One may, perhaps, in the first half of the suppression story, distinguish between Cromwell the totally ruthless uprooter and the King who had no small feeling for what was best in the religious life. But the whole position of the religious had for some years now been precarious. Some inmates seem already to have slipped quietly away, and the events of 1536 must have seemed ominous to those who remained. But it does not seem, at this stage of Henry VIII's Church policy, that total abolition was irrevocably intended. What vitiated the proceedings was the new principle, unknown to the Lancastrians, that the endowments of many monasteries and nunneries should be turned wholly away from religious uses.

It was, however, true that many of the worst and weakest religious houses, particularly a large proportion of the small Augustinian priories, were among those dissolved, with no loss to religion, in 1536. Some houses of good, or at least decent, observances were also swept away. But some of these smaller and less wealthy houses of monks and canons were excluded from this first dissolution. Such monks and canons as wished to "continue in religion" were transferred, as from Netley to Beaulieu, to larger abbeys which survived. So too many of the smaller nunneries, as at Stixwould in Lincolnshire and St Mary's at Winchester, contrived to gain exemption. It would indeed, in many areas, have been difficult for a woman to pursue a religious vocation except in a nunnery whose revenues fell below the determined £200. Many nuns, moreover, were old or unmarriageable and could have seen no future in any life but that of the cloister. The larger monasteries, including those where efficiency and observance were at their best, continued as before. They had, by now, subscribed to the royal headship of the Church. On such an understanding, as in modern Anglicanism, there could have been a place for them in Henry's ecclesiastical settlement.

What may, almost finally, have tilted the balance against the religious was the serious political unrest which burst out in the last months of 1536. The Lincolnshire Rising, and the Pilgrimage of Grace in the more northerly counties, were the strongest threat to his rule that Henry VIII ever had to face. Some monasteries, not all of them willingly but others gladly enough, became deeply involved. A few of the abbots were active supporters of the rebels, whose "platform" included no more dissolutions and the restoration of monasteries already dissolved. The religious, so it seems, were better loved in the North than nearer London. Some smaller abbeys already dissolved, among them Easby and Sawley, were reinstated by the insurgents during their short spell of local power. When the rising collapsed the restored monasteries were inevitably dissolved again. Abbots like those of Kirkstead and Jervaulx, who had caught up in the rising or who were under suspicion, were executed, and their abbeys were suppressed with no pensions for the monks such as those which had been paid elsewhere to the religious who had returned to secular life. Most monasteries in the South were tamer than those in the North; from them, except perhaps from the Carthusians, the King need never have expected the trouble caused by some in the northern province. But he had had his warning, and his fright. From 1537 onwards, with economic as well as political arguments to urge Henry on, there was little doubt that the remaining convents would be swept away.

The last, most formal blow was dealt by the Suppression Act of 1539. But before that year many monasteries and nunneries which had outlasted 1536, and all the friaries, were gradually surrendered. The greatest abbeys were those that fell at the end; the process of dissolution lasted into 1540, the last surrender being that of Waltham. The cathedral priories, except for Bath and Coventry, were duly converted into secular collegiate cathedrals. Six other religious houses had their churches turned into the secular cathedrals of new bishoprics, a small fulfilment by the king of Wolsey's idea, and of his own scheme for new sees which had at one time been more ambitious and would, among other splendid churches, have preserved that of Fountains Abbey. Two abbeys, at Thornton and Burton on Trent, were turned into secular collegiate establishments. But they, along with nearly all the other secular colleges, were in turn dissolved in the last three years of Henry's reign. The financial demands, and the requirements of lead, brought about by a war with France were a powerful influence in this new act in the ecclesiastical revolution.

Two main aspects of the suppression were the fate of

the buildings and the treatment of those who had used them.

The disposal of the monastic buildings, in an unantiquarian and unsentimental age, was ruthless to a degree; one must remember, in all fairness to the despoilers of 1539, that the alien priories, and the houses abolished by Wolsey, had fared little better. Once emptied of its monks or nuns a religious house became a mere commodity, to be realized by the Crown for what it would fetch as property, as ready for use building material, or as secondhand goods. Movable objects were sold off for what they would fetch, lead was a commodity of special interest and value, a few lecterns and sets of choir stalls were taken to neighbouring parish churches. Some tombs were transferred, as one sees at Bodmin and St Margaret's at Leicester. But most of the apparatus of monastic worship, as of the monks' daily life, was dispersed and in time disappeared. Where the grantees or buyers of monastic houses wished to make their homes in the buildings they would swiftly alter the parts they meant to use and demolish the rest. In other cases, most notably with some of the remote abbeys of the Cistercians, the buildings were left to go to ruin, and to serve as quarries for the neighbourhood. Where religious houses had stood in or near towns this process of builders' self-help would be specially fast. But at Tavistock, Eynsham, and elsewhere one hears of substantial surviving ruins in the reign of Charles II or as late as the eighteenth century.

Of greater importance was the total or partial preservation of some monastic churches. Where the nave was already used as a parish church, as at Chepstow, Nun Monkton, Dunstable, and elsewhere, its preservation was easy enough. At Pershore the parishioners exchanged the nave for the far more beautiful eastern limb, and at Tewkesbury, Romsey, and Great Malvern they obtained by purchase and by other means, the use of the whole church except for the Lady Chapel. Cartmel, Brecon, Selby, and Christchurch are other places where the whole of a monastic church most happily survives; the list printed on pages 170–180 gives fuller information on the degree to which our mediaeval monastic churches have partially or wholly survived as parish churches or cathedrals.

The treatment of the expelled religious was much illuminated, and put on a basis of reality rather than romance, by Mr Geoffrey Baskerville. The few who resisted, like the Abbots of Colchester, Reading, and Glastonbury, were executed as ruthlessly as were Henry VIII's erring wives or possible claimants to his throne. But for the great bulk of the religious their quiet transition to the secular life was made reasonably easy and financially attractive. For many, of course, the closing of their convents must have meant a hard parting from old and well tried ways. But no physical cruelty was involved, and we may dismiss the highly coloured picture of devout old men hounded out in destitution to wander cold and tearful in a harshly strange world. For most of the leading monastic figures their future was one of comfortable ease, if no longer of high responsibility. Several fitted happily into the new bishoprics and deaneries of Henry's creation. Where a leading abbot accepted no new preferment he would be allowed to live on in some large manor house with an income equivalent, in modern terms, to £3,000 or more; abbesses like those of Shaftesbury and

Wilton were no less well equipped to fill a continuing good place in county society. Prebendal stalls, benefices, and chantries were available for many who chose to take them, and when in another few years the chantries were dissolved the one-time religious took pensions like those of them who had not continued in any clerical post. At the lower levels the pensions were not lavish, but they were better than starvation and could be supplemented. Many of those who left the cloister in the 1530s in due course married, the most notable among them being Paul Bush, the first Bishop of Bristol who had been the last prior of the Bonshommes at Edington.

The really fervent spirits had mostly been eliminated by 1539, and very few of the male religious seem to have made any attempt, once driven from their cloisters, to keep together and maintain in simple privacy the bare essentials of the monastic life. With the nuns, more genuine on the whole in their vocation and without the monks' and canons' opportunities for new careers, the position was sometimes a little different. We hear, for instance, of some Wilton nuns retiring with their abbess to the fine manor in which this generously pensioned lady lived after the suppression; the private recitation of the offices, if not the public splendours of conventual High Mass, would under such conditions have been easy enough. More notable, from Denny Abbey in the Cambridgeshire fens, was the migration to her Midland home of Abbess Elizabeth Throckmorton and some of her Franciscan nuns. For in the Throckmortons' mansion of Coughton Court near Stratford-upon-Avon these sincere "votarists of St Clare" continued for some years in semi-secret religion, reciting their offices and wearing their habits in the guarded seclusion of attics and private rooms. These Poor Clares were, however, exceptional; for most of those who still yearned for the cloistered life there was nothing for it but to wait in quiet and lonely hope that one day their old homes would "be re-edified".

For these devoted spirits the day did not come till Mary I was on the throne. Even then, there were difficulties with the laymen who now possessed the old monastic sites. Those desiring to resume their vocation had been diminished by death, and for several reasons it was not till well on in the queen's short reign that a modest start could be made with a monastic restoration. But for a few years a beginning was made on the undoing of what Mary's father had brought about.

The first restorations were in 1555 when the Observant Franciscans of Greenwich went back to their old priory, and when some Carthusians from various pre-Suppression Charterhouses were resettled at Sheen. Dominicans started their activities in London, not in the old Blackfriars but in the church and surviving domestic buildings of St Bartholomew's at Smithfield. The most important Marian restoration was that of Westminster Abbey in 1556; the community was small but Abbot John Feckenham had much increased it by the time the queen died. Ideas were also afoot for the restoration of St Alban's and Glastonbury, but Mary's death came too soon for their fulfilment. The Bridgettines who had kept together in exile abroad, along with some survivors still living in England, went back to Syon in 1557. So too, after an interval at King's Langley, the Dominican nuns moved back to Dartford once the death of Anne of Cleves had freed the buildings for their use; among them was a half-sister of Bishop Fisher of Rochester who had been executed under Henry VIII.

Elizabeth I's accession in 1558 was obviously ominous for the restored monks and nuns. But they lingered on for some months, and Westminster Abbey was still a Benedictine church when the new queen was crowned there. But in the summer of 1559 the restored religious houses were again dissolved. The Carthusians, Bridgettines, and Dominican nuns made their way to the Continent, there to establish the first of the "refugee" convents which would keep open, for men and women of English birth, the facilities for living the religious life.

These English monasteries and nunneries, of necessity located abroad during penal times but drawing their inmates from England, must for various reasons be briefly mentioned here. Though their buildings are outside the scope of this book they did much to fill the gap between the monasticism of late mediaeval times and the religious houses of modern England. In a few cases, most notably with the Bridgettines, they provided an actual continuity between the two periods of monastic life. Their existence and example, moreover, were not without their influence on Anglicans and on members of other denominations.

We have seen how a few English religious communities continued their observance, after their expulsion in 1559, with little or no break. But most of the English convents of penal times took their origins from various seventeenth-century dates. These new foundations were mostly in northern France or in the Habsburg Netherlands (now Belgium). A few, however, were in Catholic areas of

Germany, while the Bridgettines eventually settled at Lisbon. The Benedictines were important in this field with their five medium-sized priories at Douai, Dieulouard in Lorraine, St Malo, Paris, and at Lamspring in central Germany. There were no refugee houses of Cistercians, Augustinian Canons, or Premonstratensians. But all the friars were represented among the English convents on the Continent. Some of these expatriate religious used buildings already existing, as at Bornhem near Antwerp where the Dominicans moved into an empty monastery of considerable size and dignity.

More numerous than the monks and friars were the nuns; by contrast to mediaeval England we are now in the time when the female religious outnumbered the men. Mediaeval England had contained no Carmelite nuns, but from 1619 onwards there came to be several Continental houses. The Benedictine nuns were well represented; there were Austin canonesses in two Belgian convents and in Paris, and in penal times there were more English convents of Poor Clares than under Henry VIII. Dominican nuns were also active, as well as the Bridgettines to whom we have already referred. Some of the English nuns abroad were, moreover, in order and congregations of new growth since the Counter-Reformation.

The peak numbers in these expatriate English convents seem to have been reached in the second half of the seventeenth century; this was certainly true of the Benedictine monks.* Numbers fell with the Georgian decline in English Catholicism. Throughout the penal period

* See Dom Hugh Aveling in *Downside Review*, Spring, 1961.

the numbers professed in these monasteries, nunneries, and friaries were remarkably high in relation to the field of recruitment. All in all, these Continental houses of English religious, along with the various English and Scots Colleges and the establishments of the English Jesuits, represented a remarkable achievement of steadfastness and devotion. In their support the English Catholic families showed great constancy and zeal – among the women at all events rather more, in many cases, than had been evident in their mediaeval equivalents. Most Catholic families of any note would send one daughter at least to some English convent abroad. One even hears, despite the difficulties imposed by distance, of postulants coming over, via the Vicar Apostolic of the London District, from Catholic families of Maryland in Colonial America.

Not all the monks and friars in these English convents abroad stayed permanently in the cloister, for many were sent to the arduous, and often dangerous, task of pastoral and missionary work in England itself. There could, however, be no question, for well over a century, of restoring conventual life in England. But James II summoned several members of the religious orders to England. For a short time their habits were worn openly at Court. Had the king's political tactics been less disastrous to himself there might, perhaps have been some degree of monastic restoration. But James's deposition came too soon for such developments. Yet the Bar Convent at York, which was established in his reign, survives to this day. The institute of The Blessed Virgin Mary, to which it belongs, had been founded, earlier in the seventeenth century, by Mary Ward, its purpose being the education of girls. An earlier foundation near York had been dispersed under the Commonwealth, and the inmates of yet another convent close to York were imprisoned at the time of the Popish Plot. Then in 1686 the present convent was started, in York itself, on its present site just outside Micklegate Bar. For many years its existence was precarious. Great care had to be taken to hide from hostile Protestants the real nature of this school for the daughters of northern Catholic gentry. The "Ladies at the Bar" wore no religious habits till after 1790. Till then, in their slate-coloured gowns with caps and hoods, they bore the appearance of "graver matrons" who lived together but who were not enclosed and could entertain friends and pay visits out in the city. Their chapel was long open to the public, and in 1786 the convent's present frontage, of red brick and with simple stone dressings like many other large York houses of the "Adam" period, was built. Once the penal laws were relaxed the life of this convent became less concealed and at the same time more similar, in such matters as dress and a private chapel, to that of the English religious now obliged, by the onset of the French Revolution, to return to a native country where their existence and corporate life were no longer illegal.

In the meantime there had been movements, among Anglicans, towards one version or another of the religious life. From the Elizabethan Settlement onwards there were, at various times, some Anglicans who felt that the complete elimination of all forms of the religious life had been too drastic a step. So in the seventeenth and eighteenth centuries there were individuals and small groups who privately led a quasi-monastic life of meditation and spiritual exercises. Among these were the two

Misses Kemeys at Clapton in Gordano not far from Bristol, their spiritual director being the famous Bishop Ken who had by this time been deprived of his Somerset bishopric. The movement, as one might expect, tended to be strongest among High Churchmen and Nonjurors.

The best known of these Anglican strivings towards the religious life was the community established in the reign of Charles I by the Laudian High Churchman Nicholas Ferrar. The experiment was made on his estate at Little Gidding in Huntingdonshire, the male and female members of the community being made up of Ferrar's own family and various relatives. It was not monastic, but it certainly was a new experiment in community life, with its members living in the house and reciting the Litany, the Prayer Book Offices, and other observances in a specially built chapel. This chapel, survives, a good deal altered since Ferrar's time and with a façade of 1714. But the fittings are many of them those used by the Little Gidding community, the Carolean stalls being arranged as in a monastic or college choir, and the whole atmosphere being eloquent still of that pioneering venture in the religious life.

Nor were the Anglicans the only non-Roman body to be influenced by the memory and example of the early religious. The Moravians, themselves a Protestant body of pre-Reformation antecedents, and with their thought and terminology deeply coloured by mediaeval Catholicism, owed not a little to the old monasticism in their famous communities at Herrnhut, Fulneck in Yorkshire, and elsewhere. Of particular interest is their use of the word *choir* to denote an organized body, for example a married men's or single sisters' choir, within a larger

159

community. Through John Wesley himself the example of these Moravian communities had an obvious effect on the early Methodists. Some of the same leanings, unconsciously deriving from various aspects of Catholic religious life, were found in groups like the Shakers who originated in England but flourished more in America. The Salvation Army, moreover, has much about it to recall the military orders, the friars, and the Sisters of Mercy.

Monastic prospects in England were dramatically changed by the relaxation of the Penal Laws and by the effects of the French Revolution. The former made legal the building of Catholic churches, including any for conventual worship. The latter not only made it necessary for many communities of English religious to return to their native land, but forced the members of some French orders to find temporary refuge in this country. Some, like the Cistercian nuns who eventually settled near Wimborne in Dorset, continued in England after it became politically possible for them to go back to France. The situation of over two centuries was exactly reversed. The Continent had long been a refuge for monks and nuns from England. Now, and later on when some French communities withdrew to England during anticlerical phases in the policy of the Third Republic, it was England that became a refuge for Continental religious. From 1793 there begins the continued story of modern monasticism in England, a country which now contains many convents of various types, and far more female religious than there were before the Reformation. The position of the religious orders is, however, in one respect very different from that which they held before the time of Henry VIII. In the Middle Ages the monasteries were an important aspect of what was then the only religious body in the field. Nowadays they are an element, albeit a vital one, in a minority denomination, or else part of one "wing" only in the Established Church.

Monasticism itself, by the time of its return to England, had also greatly changed. Many of the orders and congregations established in this country in modern times had come into being since the Counter-Reformation. The older orders had also altered considerably. The Benedictines of the English Congregation, for instance, have become more interested than they were in educational work, and their modern churches are obviously more "open" in arrangement, and less subdivided by screens and internal walls, than was the case with Benedictine churches in the Middle Ages. The Canons Regular and the friars are more concerned than in mediaeval times with ordinary parochial work, while modern Benedictine and Cistercian nuns are more contemplative and rigidly enclosed than were their Plantagenet or early Tudor opposite numbers. The inner spirit and outlook of the modern religious are not within the scope of this book, but here too the post-Tridentine changes have been profound, and monasticism has been anything but static. It was an unawareness of these facts, and a mistaken feeling that they could resume, in a more romantic spirit, from where the mediaeval religious had been interrupted, that led to many of the mistakes and disasters which befell some early Anglican experimenters in monasticism.

The refugee communities of the 1790s had often lost nearly all their money and possessions. They were therefore very poor, depended on the generosity of English friends, and at first could do little but adapt the one-time private mansions in which they were housed. One of these adapted manor houses was that of Downside, high up in the Mendip country at Stratton-on-the-Fosse. The Douai Benedictines, after a sojourn in Shropshire, bought the property in 1814. In eight more years they started the most important of the specifically monastic buildings put up by any English community in these early days of restored monastic life. The chapel and domestic buildings of this time, in a version of Early English unmistakably of this pre-Tractarian period, were by the Bath architect H. E. Goodridge who worked frequently, though not invariably, in this idiom. But the main part of England's new wave of conventual building belonged to the Victorian Gothic revival as it flourished under Pugin and those who followed him.

The beginnings of modern Anglican monasticism coincided exactly with "ecclesiology" and the revival of Gothic on supposedly mediaeval lines. The story itself, too long and complex for treatment here, is of great interest and fascination. The experience of monastic life had long been suspended, so the work was largely experimental. The new communities, whether of men or women, had to start from the beginning, many of those who initiated new ventures having little idea of the real nature of their task. Along with such great figures as John Mason Neale and Dr Pusey some curious eccentrics moved across the scene. "Fr Ignatius" Lyne of Llanthony among the men, and Priscilla Lydia Sellon the would-be "Arch-Abbess" of England are perhaps the best known. Lower down the scale there were many recruits who could never have long persevered and were

uite unsuited to the realities of monasticism – elegant
nd well-born young men who could have stepped from
he pages of a Disraeli novel or from a pre-Raphaelite
icture and for whom monasticism, with a strong empha-
is placed on its aesthetic and neo-mediaeval aspects, was
iore an attitude of mind than a true spiritual disposition.
'et much has been achieved, and in monastic or quasi-
ionastic bodies like the Society of St John the Evange-
st and the Community of the Resurrection, and in many
f its numerous sisterhoods, the Anglo-Catholics have
volved a religious life of which they can well be proud.
'heir buildings, moreover, whether they be churches or
omestic groupings, are often of real note within the
eneral corpus of Victorian or later architecture. So in
ome Anglican convents one finds vintage work by such
nportant figures as Street, Butterfield, Woodyer, Pear-
on, Bodley, and Comper. Most of this, of course, is
aryingly Gothic, but Sir Walter Tapper's House of the
Resurrection at Mirfield in Yorkshire is Romanesque,
vhile Byzantine inspiration went to the making of the
ross arches and dome of the truly beautiful chapel built
•y C. C. Thompson for the Society of the Sacred Mission
t Kelham near Newark. Church of England monasti-
ism has even produced its ruined church in the now
esolate, and never completed priory church which
erved "Father Ignatius" and his "Benedictines" at
Capel-y-Ffin, just over the Breconshire border at the head
•f the Llanthony valley. The monastery buildings, after
everal changes of occupation and ownership, are now
 guest house. The eastern half of the church, closely
iodelled in style on the late twelfth-century Transitional
•riory whose ruins are a little way down the valley, was

designed by an architect named Charles Buckeridge. I[t] is unroofed now and convincingly desolate. Its furnish[-] ings have gone (some stallwork being now in use a[t] Prinknash), but the founder's tomb remains, amid weed[s] and hideous Victorian tiles, in the empty choir. Alon[g] with the splendidly mediaeval ruin of *Lantonia Prima* this wreck of its eccentric founder's hopes makes thi[s] lovely, mountain-girt valley of the Honddhu the choices[t] locality in all Wales and England for the perambulato[r] of priories.

Most of the religious houses in modern England ar[e] those of the Roman obedience. As many communities[,] particularly of nuns and Sisters of Mercy, live in con[-] verted mansions there are many establishments whos[e] architecture is not specifically conventual. Where plan[s] of a more obviously monastic type have been chose[n] the churches and other buildings of the Victorian perio[d] are apt to contain work by such prolific designers a[s] C. F. Hansom and the various Pugins. Domestic build[-] ings, whether of monasteries, nunneries, or friaries, ten[d] (as generally in the Catholic world since the Counter[-] Reformation) to differ much from their mediaeval fore[-] runners. There is, for instance, a greater emphasis o[n] the private room or cell as distinct from the dormitory[,] while cloisters, if they exist at all, are far less impor[-] tant than in the days when they were used as living an[d] working space. Refectories, on the other hand, are ap[t] to be much as they were, but other domestic apartment[s] have moved with the times. We must, in this brief an[d] final survey, speak mainly of monks' churches, for man[y] of these (though not the large French Gothic church o[f] he modern Carthusians at Parkminster in Sussex) can eadily be visited.

As among the Anglican religious the overwhelming majority of these churches are in one version or another of Gothic. Their architecture is that of the nineteenth-and early twentieth-century period in which they were designed; some are consciously modelled, with some differences of detail, on England's mediaeval abbeys and priories. So at Ramsgate Pugin designed a Benedictine church, and its attendant buildings, which were an important statement of the Gothic Revival as evangelically proclaimed by himself. Another Pugin work, started in its architect's life and finished, with some modifications, in the 1930s, is the large Cistercian abbey church of Mount St Bernard in Leicestershire. It is "Early English" in style, and with an eastern limb much longer than most of those built by the same order in its early days in England, Ireland, and elsewhere. A few years later, at Woodchester in the Cotswolds, the spread-out buildings of C. F. Hansom's new Passionist (now Dominican) priory were reasonably convincing, but the church with its short chancel comes nearer to the "parochial" conception of design. So too, modern friary churches like those of the Servites and Carmelites in Kensington have little to distinguish them from ordinary parish churches. At Leicester, however, the recently completed Dominican church, mock-Perpendicular in style and with a slightly more modern idiom in its nave, is cruciform and more "monastic" in character. The private altars in a church of present-day religious are sometimes provided more simply and functionally than they were in the more spacious Norman or early Gothic days; one sees this at Blackfriars in Oxford and in the Sussex priory of the Premonstratensians at Storrington.

Our last passage must be on some of the Benedictine monasteries which have been built in England since early last century. With Benedictine houses our record begins; with the Benedictines of our own time we fitly end.

At Belmont near Hereford the abbey church, by Edward Pugin, was built in a somewhat early Victorian manner, cruciform with a central tower and with each of its two main limbs of nearly equal length. At Ampleforth too the first Gothic buildings were early in the Victorian tradition, but the church has now been replaced by that designed by Sir Giles Gilbert Scott. It has a central high altar, the monks being on one side and the boys of the school on the other, and its Gothic has an idiom of our own century. At Buckfast the new church, on the foundations of the mediaeval Cistercian one, is aesthetically less happy than these others, Franco-Lotharingian idioms having been mixed with more English references. Largest and most stately of all is the great church at Downside, with its unfinished neo-Perpendicular nave by Sir Giles Gilbert Scott – the final element in a church whose styles also include an unhappily ornate transept of the 1870s and a superb early twentieth-century choir by T. H. Garner who had been Bodley's partner. The post-Goodridge domestic and school buildings are also a slowly accumulated and interesting mixture, ending with some admirable Arts and Crafts Gothic boarding houses by Leonard Stokes and some recently finished, "contemporary" school buildings by Lionel Brett. It is in the school buildings attached to such educational abbeys, and to convents of teaching nuns, that one is so far most likely to find modern English religious houses using contemporary buildings.

More exotic in their English setting, both of them started for monks from France, and both of them buildings of great character, are the abbeys at the Hampshire Farnborough and Quarr in the Isle of Wight.

Originally built by the exiled Empress Eugenie as the burial church for Napoleon III, the Prince Imperial, and herself, the church at Farnborough is of a deeper historic interest than most modern abbeys in England. High perched on a hilltop as befits a church dedicated to St Michael, it was finished by 1887 when some Premonstratensians came to care for the tombs and maintain services in the church; in a few years these white canons were replaced by French Benedictines who have recently been succeeded by a colony from Prinknash. French Flamboyant in its basic style, the church was designed by Gabriel Destailleur who had restored various châteaux in France, and who had also built château-style mansions for the Rothschilds in Vienna and at Waddesdon in Buckinghamshire. The building is capped, a little incongruously, with a dome in the manner of the Renaissance.

Continental inspiration, of a very different type, appears also in the challenging set of buildings put up, between 1908 and 1912, at Quarr. The church, in particular, shows most impressive groupings in Flemish brick; Flemish too is the motivation of the other buildings. But a few antiquarian details apart the modern Gothic designs by Dom Paul Bellot, a French architect who had become a Benedictine, were simple and "advanced" for their date.

167

We come, at the last, to English monasticism in our own time. Institutionally, it is alive in a way that Henry VIII and his immediate successors could scarcely have foreseen. Architecturally, however, it has so far been mainly rooted in its mediaeval past; whether Anglican or Catholic the new buildings needed for this revived aspect of church life were built at a time when little else was likely. So far, one notes, there are no English equivalents to Le Corbusier's hillside Dominican friary of La Tourette in France, or to the work of Mr Marcel Breuer in the vast Benedictine abbey of St John at Collegeville in Minnesota.* A great chance exists, however, for monastic designers in this century (and perhaps in the next) on the steep, superbly scenic Cotswold slopes now occupied by the Benedictines of Prinknash.

It was in 1928 that the Benedictines of Caldey Island came to the old Cotswold manor house which had once belonged to the abbots of Gloucester. A few years later designs were made, on a visionary, Cluny-like scale, for a huge abbey church and extensive domestic buildings. The steeply sloping site was most unpromising for such a venture, but the late Mr H. S. Goodhart Rendel got out plans. These involved the most elaborate foundations and underpinning at the church's liturgical eastern end, and assumed that construction would be by traditional methods, with great masses of load-bearing concrete, brick, and stone. The great church's ground-plan would in the main be cruciform and traditionally mediaeval, while the style would be a sort of Byzantino-Romanesque, with some Durham details in the crypt and elements of Cluny or Vézelay in the narthex. The

* For this, see *Architectural Forum* and *Architectural Record*, November, 1961

168

steepness of the site made it necessary to have not one crypt but two, one above the other. A start was made in 1939. War imposed delays. Slow building has since proceeded. Colossal foundations have been imposed on the Prinknash slopes, and above them the sub-crypt is now nearly complete.

One may reasonably doubt that the scheme of 1939 was ever very relevant, artistically speaking, to our own century; the Anglican cathedrals at Liverpool and Guildford are really the swansongs of that tradition. What is now quite clear is that the project is a wild stylistic anachronism and that financially it is a fantasy. The Abbot of Prinknash has much the same problem as that faced by the Archbishop of Liverpool, and it seems mercifully unlikely that the abbey as so far planned will ever be built. New and simple monastery buildings are urgently needed for a growing Prinknash community, and for some years to come the sub-crypt can amply serve the monks as their church. The great chance will come, perhaps next century, when the time is reached for a new and truly "contemporary" abbey church. This could, one feels, be built partly at least on the platform of the existing crypt; what will really matter will be the talent of the chosen architect and the up-to-date inventiveness of his design. The splendid site has its distant view of the Malverns, and of the rich Severn vale which was once so eminent a centre of Benedictine monasticism. It looks easily down to Gloucester's great abbey church which was more than once in the vanguard of English mediaeval achitecture. Here, one can now hope, some abbey designer of the future will give modern English monasticism its contemporary architectural expression.

Appendix

A LIST OF THE MORE IMPORTANT REMAINS OF MEDIAEVAL RELIGIOUS HOUSES

*Denotes the fact that all or part of the fabric is under the care of the Ministry of Works and is readily accessible to the public.

A. Augustinian Canons. B. Benedictines.Bons.Bonshommes. C. Cistercians. Car. Carthusians. Cl. Cluniacs. G. Gilbertines Gr. Grammontines. Hosp. Knights Hospitallers. P. Premonstatensians. Tem. Templars. A.P. Alien Priory. F. Friary. N. Nunnery (*e.g.* B.N.=Benedictine Nuns).

BEDFORDSHIRE

A.	Dunstable Priory	Nave in use
B.N.	Elstow Abbey	Nave in use

BERKSHIRE

B.	Abingdon Abbey	Remains of domestic buildings
B.	Hurley Priory	Church in use
B.	Reading Abbey	Ruins

BUCKINGHAMSHIRE

A.	Chetwode Priory	Parts of church in use
C.	Medmenham Abbey	Ruins

CAMBRIDGESHIRE AND ISLE OF ELY

A.	Cambridge, Barnwell Priory	Gate chapel and domestic remains
B.	Cambridge, Buckingham College	Court survives in Magdalene College

B.N.	Cambridge, St Radegund's Priory	Church and buildings survive in Jesus College
F.	Cambridge, Dominican Priory	Considerable remains in Emmanuel College
Fr.N*	Denny Abbey	Important remains
B.	Ely Cathedral	Church and many domestic remains
B.	Thorney Abbey	Most of nave in use

CHESHIRE

B.	Birkenhead Priory	In ruins; chapter house now a chapel
B.	Chester Cathedral (formerly Abbey)	Church and splendid domestic remains
A.	Norton Priory	Slight remains

CORNWALL

A.	St Germans Priory	Nave in use
A.P.	St Michael's Mount	Church and other buildings survive

CUMBERLAND

C.	Calder Abbey	Extensive ruins
A.	Carlisle Cathedral	Church, refectory, undercroft
C.	Holm Cultram Abbey	Part of nave in use
A.	Lanercost Priory	Nave in use; * choir and buildings ruined

DEVON

C.	Buckland Abbey	Church remains as a mansion (now a branch of the Plymouth City Museum)
B.N.	Exeter, Polslo Priory	Considerable domestic remains

B.	Exeter, St Nicholas' Priory	Part of buildings
A.	Frithelstock Priory	Considerable ruins
B.	Tavistock Abbey	Considerable remains
P.	Torquay, Torre Abbey	Important remains

DORSET

B.	*Abbotsbury Abbey	Ruins, barn, and chapel
C.	Bindon Abbey	Some remains
C.	Forde Abbey	Important remains in mansion
B.	Milton Abbey	Choir and transepts in use
B.	Sherborne Abbey	Church in use; buildings incorporated in Sherborne School

DURHAM

B.	Durham Cathedral	Church and very notable domestic remains
B.	*Finchale Priory	Ruins
B.	*Jarrow Priory	Claustral remains

ESSEX

B.	Colchester Abbey	Ruins
A.	*Colchester, St Botolph's Priory	Ruins of nave
A.	Little Dunmow Priory	Part of church in use
A.	St Osyth's Priory	Buildings now a mansion
Cl.	Southend, Prittlewell Priory	Important remains
A.	Waltham Abbey	Nave in use. *Gatehouse, etc.

GLOUCESTERSHIRE (INCLUDING BRISTOL)

A.	Bristol Cathedral (formerly Abbey)	Part of church, chapter house, other domestic remains

172

B.	Bristol, St James's Priory	Nave in use
F.	Bristol, Dominican Priory	Important domestic remains
B.	Deerhurst Priory	Nave of church in use
C.	Flaxley Abbey	Important domestic remains
B.	Gloucester Cathedral (formerly Abbey)	Church and particularly important domestic remains
F.	Gloucester, Dominican Priory	Part of church a house; very important domestic remains
F.	Gloucester, Franciscan Priory	Part of church remains
A.	Gloucester, St Oswald's Priory	Ruins of church
C.	Hayles Abbey	Ruins
C.	Kingswood Abbey	Fine gatehouse; slight other remains
B.	Leonard Stanley Priory	Church in use
B.	Tewkesbury Abbey	Church in use

HAMPSHIRE

C.	Beaulieu Abbey	Ruins and most of west range; refectory the parish church
A.	Christchurch Priory	Church in use
C.	Netley Abbey	Important ruins
A.P.	Pamber Priory	Part of church in use
B.N.	Romsey Abbey	Church in use
P.	*Titchfield Abbey	Extensive remains
B.	Winchester Cathedral	Church, no domestic remains of note

HEREFORDSHIRE

A.N.	Aconbury Priory	Part of church in use

173

Gr.	Craswall Priory	Interesting ruins
C.	Dore Abbey	Presbytery and transepts in use
A.	Flanesford Priory	Considerable remains
B.	Leominster Priory	Nave in use

HERTFORDSHIRE

A.	Royston Priory	Part of church in use
B.	St Albans Cathedral (formerly Abbey)	Church; splendid gateway

KENT

F.	Aylesford, Carmelite Friary	Important remains; recently re-occupied by Carmelites
P.	Bradsole Abbey (near Dover)	Important ruins
B.	Canterbury, Cathedral	Church and many monastic buildings
B.	*Canterbury, St Augustine's Abbey	Gateways and other remains
F.	Canterbury, Dominican Friary	Considerable remains
B.	Dover Priory	Guest house and refectory incorporated in Dover College
B.N.	Malling Abbey	Important ruins; site now occupied by Anglican Benedictine nuns
B.N.	Minster in Sheppey	Church in use
B.	Rochester Cathedral	Church and some domestic ruins

LANCASHIRE

A.	Cartmel Priory	Church in use; gateway
P.	Cockersand Abbey	Ruined except chapter-house

174

C.	*Furness Abbey	Extensive remains
B.	Upholland Priory	Choir in use as church
C.	Whalley Abbey	Extensive ruins; gate-houses

LEICESTERSHIRE

| A. | Owston Abbey | Part of church in use |
| A. | Ulverscroft Priory | Important ruins |

LINCOLNSHIRE

A.	Bourn Priory	Nave in use
B.	Crowland Abbey	Part of nave in use; impressive remains
B.	Deeping St James Priory	Nave in use
B.	Freiston Priory	Nave in use
C.	Kirkstead Abbey	Gate chapel in use
A.	*Thornton Abbey	Ruins; fine gateway

LONDON

B.N.	Bishopsgate, St Helen's	Church in use
Car.	Charterhouse	Important remains; chapter house now chapel
Hosp.	Clerkenwell, St John's Priory	Crypt of choir, gateway
A.	Smithfield, St Bartholomew's Priory	Presbytery in use
A.	Southwark Cathedral (formerly Priory of St Mary Overy)	Transepts and choir; nave modern
Tem.	Temple Church	Church now restored after bombing
B.	Westminster Abbey	Church; monastic buildings

NORFOLK

| B. | *Binham Priory | Nave in use |
| Cl. | *Castle Acre Priory | Important remains |

B.	Norwich Cathedral	Church, cloisters, domestic remains
F.	Norwich, Dominican Friary	Church now a public hall
Cl.	*Thetford Priory	Extensive remains
A.	Walsingham Priory	Ruins
B.	Wymondham Abbey	Nave in use

NORTHAMPTONSHIRE

| A. | Canons Ashby Priory | Nave in use |
| B. | Peterborough Cathedral (formerly Abbey) | Church; few domestic remains |

NORTHUMBERLAND

P.	Blanchland Abbey	Nave and transept in use; gateway
A.	Brinkburn Priory	Church complete
A.	Hexham Priory	Church in use (modern nave)
B.	*Lindisfarne Priory	Extensive ruins
F.	Newcastle, Dominican Friary	Considerable remains
B.	*Tynemouth Priory	Extensive ruins

NOTTINGHAMSHIRE

B.	Blyth Priory	Nave in use
A.	Mattersey Priory	Ruins of church and buildings
A.	Newstead Priory	Now a private mansion
C.	*Rufford Abbey	Claustral remains
A.	Thurgarton Priory	Part of nave in use
A.	Worksop Priory	Nave in use; gateway

OXFORDSHIRE

| A. | Dorchester Abbey | Church in use |
| A. | Oxford Cathedral (formerly St Frideswide's Priory) | Most of church; some domestic buildings in Christ Church |

176

B.	Oxford, Durham Hall	Some buildings survive in Trinity College
B.	Oxford, Gloucester Hall	Buildings survive in Worcester College
C.	Oxford, St Bernard's College	Buildings survive in St John's College

SHROPSHIRE

C.	*Buildwas Abbey	Extensive ruins
A.	*Haughmond Priory	Extensive ruins
A.	Lilleshall Abbey	Extensive remains
Cl.	Much Wenlock Priory	Splendid remains
B.	Shrewsbury Abbey	Nave in use

SOMERSET

B.	Bath Abbey (formerly Cathedral Priory)	Church in use
C.	Cleeve Abbey	Important domestic remains
B.	Dunster Priory	Nave in use
B.	Glastonbury Abbey	Considerable remains
Car.	Hinton Charterhouse Priory	Some remains
B.	*Muchelney Abbey	Domestic remains
A.	Stavordale Priory	Church survives as a house
A.P.	Stogursey Priory	Church in use
Car.	Witham Priory	Gate chapel in parochial use
A.	Woodspring Priory	Part of church now a house

STAFFORDSHIRE

| C. | *Croxden Abbey | In ruins |
| B. | Tutbury Priory | Nave in use |

SUFFOLK

| B. | *Bury St Edmund's Abbey | Ruins; fine gateways |

P.	Leiston Abbey	Considerable remains
A.	*St Olave's Priory,	Fine crypt

SURREY

A.	Newark Priory	Ruins
C.	Waverley Abbey	In ruins

SUSSEX

A.P.	Arundel Priory (later collegiate)	Church in use; choir privately owned
B.	Battle Abbey	Remains now a school; fine gateway
P.	*Bayham Abbey	Extensive ruins
F.	Chichester, Franciscan Friary	Choir survives
A.N.	Easebourne Priory	Church in use

WARWICKSHIRE

A.	Maxstoke Priory	Tower and gateway
C.	Merevale Abbey	Gate chapel in use
Tem.	Temple Balsall	Church (later that of Hospitallers) in use

WESTMORLAND

P.	*Shap Abbey	In ruins; tower left

WILTSHIRE

Bons.	Edington Priory	Church in use
A.N.	Lacock Abbey	Fine buildings now a mansion (National Trust)
B.	Malmesbury Abbey	Nave in use

WORCESTERSHIRE

B.	Evesham Abbey	Ruins; fine bell tower
B.	Great Malvern Priory	Church in use
P.	Halesowen Abbey	Ruins
B.	Little Malvern Priory	Part of church in use

B.	Pershore Abbey	Presbytery, one transept, and tower in use
B.	Worcester Cathedral	Church and very fine Monastic remains

YORKSHIRE

A.	Bolton Priory	Nave in use; choir in ruins
A.	Bridlington Priory	Nave in use; gateway
C.	*Byland Abbey	In ruins
P.	Coverham Abbey	In ruins
P.	*Easby Abbey	Extensive ruins
P.	*Egglestone Abbey	In ruins
C.	Fountains Abbey	Splendid ruins
A.	*Guisborough Priory	Ruins
C.	Jervaulx Abbey	Extensive ruins
A.	*Kirkham Priory	Ruined; gateway
C.	Kirkstall Abbey	Splendid ruins
G.	Malton Priory	Nave in use
B.	*Monk Bretton Priory	In ruins
Car.	*Mount Grace Priory	Very important ruins
B.N.	Nun Monkton Priory	Nave in use
C.	*Rievaulx Abbey	Splendid ruins
C.	Roche Abbey	Considerable ruins
C.	*Sawley Abbey	Considerable remains
B.	Selby Abbey	Church in use
C.N.	Swine Priory	Choir of church in use
G.	Watton Priory	Site excavated; Prior's lodging inhabited
B.	*Whitby Abbey	Considerable ruins
B.	York, St. Mary's Abbey	Ruins, fortifications
B.	York, Holy Trinity Priory	Nave in use

WALES AND MONMOUTHSHIRE
(T. = Order of Tiron)

B.	Abergavenny Priory, Monmouthshire	Church in use

179

C.	*Basingwerk Abbey, Flintshire	Ruins
B.	Brecon Cathedral (formerly Priory)	Church in use
F.	Brecon, Dominican Friary	Choir in use as chapel of Christ College; other remains
T.	Caldy Is., Pembrokeshire	Church used by the Cistercians of modern abbey
B.	Chepstow Priory, Monmouthshire	Nave in use
C.	*Cymmer Abbey, Merionethshire	Ruins
B.	Ewenny Priory, Glamorganshire	Nave in use; remainder of church survives, also fortified precinct
A.	Llanthony Priory, Monmouthshire	Very important ruins
C.	Margam Abbey, Glamorganshire	Most of nave in use; ruins
C.	*Neath Abbey, Glamorganshire	Ruins
A.	Penmon Priory, Anglesey	Part of church in use, modern chancel
T.	St Dogmael's Abbey, Pembrokeshire	Ruins of church
C.	*Strata Florida Abbey, Cardiganshire	Some remains
P.	*Talley Abbey, Carmarthenshire	Ruins
C.	*Tintern Abbey, Monmouthshire	Extensive and important ruins
B.N.	Usk Priory, Monmouthshire	Nave in use, gatehouse
C.	*Valle Crucis Abbey, Denbighshire	Considerable remains

A Booklist

In compiling a short new booklist for the revised edition of this book I have confined myself to the mention of books of general application, and those dealing with orders as a whole rather than with individual religious houses. There is, of course, a very large amount of literature on individual monasteries, or on those of limited areas. The original author of this work, being a resident of Chester, paid particular attention to works on religious houses in Cheshire, Staffordshire, and further North. Numerous monographs also exist on religious houses in other parts of the country; some of them, on Tavistock, Winchcombe, and Leicester for example, are of recent appearance. In addition, there are many important articles and ground plans in various learned publications (particularly in *Archaeologia* and "The Archaeological Journal"), in the proceedings and transactions of county Record, Archaeological, and Historical Societies, in the appropriate volumes of the Victoria County History, and elsewhere. In many places, particularly where a ruined monastery is under the care of the Ministry of Works, excellent guidebooks can be obtained on the spot.

Turning for a moment to the more general works, one can safely say that the whole subject has been put in a new perspective by the work of Professor David Knowles and his various colleagues and assistants; a particularly full bibliography is in each of Professor Knowles's volumes on *The Religious Orders in England*.

B.D.G.L.

Sir William Dugdale (ed.), *Monasticon Anglicanum*, 6 vols, 1817–30

Abbot (later Cardinal) F. A. Gasquet, *English Monastic Life*, 1904

A. Hamilton Thompson, *English Monasteries*, 1913

D. H. S. Cranage, *The Home of the Monk*, 1926

M. R. James, *Abbeys* (i.e. those in the area served by the Great Western Railway), 1926

R. H. Snape, *English Monastic Finance* in the Later Middle Ages, 1926

Rose Graham, *English Ecclesiastical Studies*, 1929

G. G. Coulton, *Five Centuries of Religion*, 4 vols, 1929–50

R. Liddesdale Palmer, *English Monasteries in the Middle Ages*, 1930

R. E. Swartwout, *The Monastic Craftsman*, 1932

Geoffrey Baskerville, *English Monks and the Suppression of the Monasteries*, 1937

David Knowles, *The Monastic Order in England*, 1940

David Knowles, *The Religious Orders in England*, 3 vols, 1948, 1955, 1959

David Knowles and J. K. St Joseph, *Monastic Sites from the Air*, 1952

David Knowles and R. N. Hadcock, *Mediaeval Religious Houses in England and Wales*, 1953

R. Gilyard–Beer, *Abbeys*, 1958

G. H. Cook, *English Monasteries in the Middle Ages*, 1961

J. C. Dickinson, *Monastic Life in Mediaeval England*, 1961

L. F. Salzmann, *Mediaeval Building in England*, 1952

Peter Anson, *The Religious Orders and Congregations of Great Britain and Ireland*, 1949

Peter Anson, *The Call of the Cloister* (on Anglican communities), 1955

A. M. Allchin, *The Silent Rebellion* (Anglican Communities, 1845–1900), 1958

Rose Graham, *St Gilbert of Sempringham and the Gilbertines*, 1903

A. G. Little, *Studies in English Franciscan History*, 1917

Edward Hutton, *The Franciscans in England*, 1926

A. R. Martin, *Franciscan Architecture in England*, 1937

Bede Jarrett, *The English Dominicans*, 1921, 2nd edn., 1937

R. F. Bennett, *The Early Dominicans*, 1937

Aubrey Gwynn, *The English Austin Friars in the time of Wyclif*, 1940

Lancelot C. Sheppard, *The English Carmelites*, 1943

E. Margaret Thompson, *The Carthusian Order in England*, 1930

J. C. Dickinson, *The Origins of the Austin Canons*, 1950

H. M. Colvin, *The White Canons in England*, 1951

Eileen Power, *Mediaeval English Nunneries*, 1922

Index

The references in **heavy type** are to the figure-numbers of the illustrations